"If you are ready to be set free from the nagging stress of feeling chronically overwhelmed, then *Rest Now* is the book you have been looking for. Filled with practical takeaways and transformational ideas, it is sure to gain a place at the top of your favorite books list."

Mandy Arioto, president and CEO of MOPS International

"We all need a friend who understands the struggles of life. More importantly, we need a friend who points us to Jesus. Kelly Balarie does both in *Rest Now*. With transparent and tender compassion, Kelly shows us how to access the peace of God—as well as His joy—even in the midst of chaos."

Joanna Weaver, author of *Having a Mary Heart in a Martha World*

"I jumped at the chance to read *Rest Now*—not just because Kelly Balarie is known for her positive encouragement but because *I am so tired*. God's true rest eludes me. If I'm being honest, I am so far from living in that place that I don't even know how to aspire to it. *Rest Now* is full of practical advice for identifying the lies we tell ourselves that keep us from being able to embrace rest, as well as straightforward tips for overcoming the barriers we've put in the way of getting there—and ways to implement boundaries so we can remain there. This book shows us we can have that beautiful, peaceful life of rest God promised. Not someday. Not later. *Now.*"

Kelly O'Dell Stanley, author of *Praying Upside Down,*
Designed to Pray, and *InstaPrayer: Prayers to Share*

"In *Rest Now*, Kelly Balarie provides a real-life and applicable antidote for all who find themselves shuffling for approval in the pursuit of *more, busy,* and *perfection*: the ability and the wisdom to rest in the here and now, knowing we were made for this life by a God who simply wants us to *rest in His arms* when we feel weary."

Kara Lawler, author of *Everywhere Holy: Seeing Beauty,*
Remembering Your Identity, and Finding God Right Where You Are

"Kelly helps you dig deep into why you may not be experiencing *true* rest. She lovingly walks you through practical and biblical solutions to get the kind of rest that brings about transformation, freedom, and success. This book is a must-read!"

Rebecca Garcia, founder of Christian Women Entrepreneurs Network

"Reading Kelly's book reminds me of the beautiful relationship between sisters—with Kelly taking the role of a spiritual sister for her readers. She guides us through pages of wisdom and personal stories. Most evident is her heart for listening. In each chapter, Kelly brilliantly identifies challenges, applies a biblical solution, and assigns an action plan. Her book will impact several generations. Perfect for mentoring, book clubs, or small group discussions."

Christine Abraham, founder and executive director of Bible Cafe Ministries, BibleCafe.org

"Rest has always been a recurring theme in my life. No matter the season I am in—wife, mother, entrepreneur—God reminds me of His gift of rest. Then Kelly comes along in her book to remind me rest is for *now* and not just for later. This book helped me to understand total rest in God includes boundaries for myself and others. I am encouraged by knowing I can set boundaries, seize joy, and rest in God. Thank you, Kelly, for this much-needed book for the body of Christ."

Roshanda "The Rosho Live" Pratt, storyteller, live video strategist, and producer

"The fact is, I didn't want to rest now. I felt like I was bad at it. I'd rather run my furious race on the hamster wheel of life and skip the inner soul work. But Kelly has a way of cheering us on and leading us to healthier practices. There's no one more gracious and loving to encourage us toward greater peace and joy."

Melanie Dale, author of *Calm the H*ck Down*

"Full of practical application and a few touches of 'ouch' from conviction, *Rest Now* partners with the Holy Spirit for specific wisdom and boundaries to be able to navigate and put wholehearted focus, effort, and work into what God is calling us to build. This book has me declaring its truths aloud and asking for forgiveness when I feel a check in my spirit."

Adrienne Young, author of *Declare & Establish, Women Who War*, and *Don't Go Thrifting Without Me*

"In *Rest Now*, Kelly Balarie's unique gift of storytelling, relevant spiritual insight, and raw humanity beautifully collide. The result is a deep and wide panorama of Christian self-care for hurried and harried souls. From the very first lines of the introduction, you feel her brand of authenticity. The lessons are fresh. The approach is practical. The spiritual impact will be deep. So, get ready to be redirected and restored to strength in Christ as you revel in Kelly's hard-won truths. Don't wait! Read it and you will surely rest now. It's time!"

Marlinda Ireland, DMin, cofounder of Christ Church Rockaway & Montclair, New Jersey

"There are few writers who resonate with my understanding of life and the joys and challenges of truly desiring the life God created us for like Kelly Balarie. Kelly writes in a way that makes me think that she has been 'in my head' or 'reading my mail.' When I read her, I hear Kelly's voice as if she is speaking the words to me. And as she shares about herself, she somehow holds up a mirror so I see myself in most of her own stories and circumstances. I sat down to read *Rest Now* and ended up feeling like it *read me*. Kelly outlines practical pathways to live a life of rest and renewal that will satisfy the most restless of souls through some of the least-practiced spiritual disciplines—along with showing us how to create boundaries that help us maintain a lifestyle of rest that represents the life Jesus intended for us. This book is a gift for all of us who are *becoming*."

Dan McCandless, pastor of leadership development, Black Rock Church

"This book speaks right to the heart of this recovering prodigal who spent many years trying to make up for past mistakes. Kelly reminds us that doing or being more isn't the way we get to deep, soulful peace. Instead, it comes from intimately knowing God, knowing who He says we are, and learning to resist anything that tries to corrupt either of those things. It's a must-read for any Christian woman, especially those in leadership!"

Angela J. Herrington, MA, LSCC, online pastor and life coach

"Kelly opens our eyes to the emptiness of the culture's attempts to fill our God-shaped vacuum with more people, possessions, or position, and she gives us biblical and practical steps leading us to the only One who can—Jesus."

Sharon Jaynes, bestselling author of *Enough: Silencing the Lies That Steal Your Confidence*

"Rest seems like it should be simple, yet why is it so evasive? Perhaps it is because we have a one-dimensional view of what rest means and how to experience it. In *Rest Now*, Kelly brings her honest, enlightening, and refreshing perspective on how to make rest our reality. With heartfelt prayers and practical application, she leaves readers equipped and encouraged to rest."

Lisa Bishop, director of women's ministry at Park Community Church in Chicago, IL, and founder of Living a Life Unleashed LLC, doyoulalu.com

"Not only is this book engaging and well written but it also taps into the universal weariness that's numbed American society. As Kelly beautifully reminds us, there is hope—hope to overcome the fear, anxiety, and depression defining our generation through the strength and love of Christ. With humility, real-life stories, and actionable steps, Kelly shows us how to make rest a natural rhythm of life and reclaim our joy. She leads us to a place of peace that speaks to the soul."

Kari Kampakis, author of *Love Her Well: 10 Ways to Find Joy and Connection with Your Teenage Daughter* and *10 Ultimate Truths Girls Should Know*

*rest
now*

rest now

7 WAYS TO SAY NO, SET BOUNDARIES, AND SEIZE JOY

KELLY BALARIE

BakerBooks
a division of Baker Publishing Group
Grand Rapids, Michigan

© 2020 by Kelly Balarie

Published by Baker Books
a division of Baker Publishing Group
PO Box 6287, Grand Rapids, MI 49516-6287
www.bakerbooks.com

Printed in the United States of America

Library of Congress Cataloging-in-Publication Data
Names: Balarie, Kelly, 1978– author.
Title: Rest now : 7 ways to say no, set boundaries, and seize joy / Kelly Balarie.
Description: Grand Rapids, Michigan : Baker Books, a division of Baker Publishing Group, 2020.
Identifiers: LCCN 2020014918 | ISBN 9780801094972 (paperback)
Subjects: LCSH: Rest—Religious aspects—Christianity. | Habit breaking—Religious aspects—Christianity. | Simplicity—Religious aspects—Christianity.
Classification: LCC BV4597.55 .B35 2020 | DDC 248.4–dc23
LC record available at https://lccn.loc.gov/2020014918

978-1-5409-0116-3 (casebound)

Italics and/or boldface added to Scripture quotations represent the author's emphasis.

The author is represented by MacGregor & Luedeke Literary Agency.

Some names and details have been changed to protect the privacy of the individuals involved.

20 21 22 23 24 25 26   7 6 5 4 3 2 1

green press INITIATIVE

God, You know I don't do things perfectly,
but You love and want me anyway.
For this, I am grateful.
May my imperfect words
be a blessing unto You.

contents

11

introduction

REST IS NOW

> I am leaving you with a gift—peace of mind and heart.
> And the peace I give is a gift the world cannot give. So
> don't be troubled or afraid.
>
> Jesus (John 14:27)

I've always wanted rest. But I've never known how fully to get it—or live from it, for that matter.

I grew up as the oldest of six kids. I was the responsible kid, the in-charge one. I knew what needed to get done and how to accomplish it. Birth order demanded this—or so it seemed. When summer break ended, I reminded my mom of everything on the school supply checklist, ensuring nothing was forgotten. When a family member was unhappy, I sat with them to comfort them. When a sibling had a problem, it was my problem too.

One sister made a habit of skipping school. Because we attended the same high school, I constantly checked on her. I missed my classes to make sure she attended hers. It didn't make any sense; I was doing what she was doing. Either way, I was going to keep her in line. One time I got all up in her face because she was hanging out with the wrong people. I pushed her up against a cabinet and yelled in her face.

Taking care of everyone will always take its toll, emotionally. It certainly took a lot out of me. I just wanted my siblings to go "the right way." I cared a whole awful lot—or so I convinced myself.

Around the college years, my second-oldest sister said she was moving to Hawaii. I remember how jealousy came over me. It was so easy for her. So simple. She could just up and go. I couldn't leave. Who would take care of everyone? There were people in my house who needed taking care of—or so I thought. How could I leave them? Abandon them? Not be there for them?

The responsible side of me said that things would not be okay without me. That I wouldn't be okay if they were not okay. Now I see that maybe this was just the prideful side of me talking.

Around this time, I developed an eating disorder. I don't know why. My parents loved me. I had a great family. But I became a nervous wreck. I spent hours in the computer lab searching for the "perfect" job. I tirelessly worked to achieve all that was expected of me. I drove myself hard.

Finally, rather than jealously wanting other people's lives, I moved—to California. There, I still struggled with an eating disorder. To make matters worse, I got myself that "perfect" job but hated it. The issues started with the interview. I acted like their ideal candidate. I studied the company's web page. I projected everything they wanted to hear. But whoever I pretended to be—it wasn't me. It was an idealized version of their dream employee. The interviewers loved me and hired me, but I hated every second of that job. I hated the fear I felt because I had to be someone else. I hated the stress. The work was boring and headachy and required long hours. Tiring. Monotonous.

I just went on, acting like someone I wasn't. One of the worst tortures of life, I'm convinced, is being anyone other than who God created you to be.

It's just what people do, isn't it? You do what you do—until you hate life and can't bear it anymore.

I left the job after a year. Following that, I bounced around from job to job and idea to idea. *I could be a real estate agent. No, I'll be a waitress. No, I'll work in technology. No, I'll start up my own business. No, I'll blog about food. No, I'll start chef's dinners that travel all over the nation.*

Then I landed in a position doing corporate work. Rest seemed like being really great at things. Getting to a certain level. Being my "best self" and "living my best life," or something like that. So I aimed to perform at peak levels. I went all-out. But this was not rest. It always demanded more.

Later in life, I swung in the opposite direction of hard work. I powered everything down. I laid around. I stopped talking to as many people. I prayed or thought about things almost all day. But my mind got restless.

This wasn't real rest either.

15

Real Rest?

What was "real" rest? That is what my heart was after. I had to know.

I now knew what rest was not. It was not looking successful. It was not appearing good to others. It was not physically sitting. It was not abandoning everything I was responsible for. It was not being loved or wanted by people. It was not more TV and less hassles. It was not getting another person to change.

Real rest, I always thought, was "out there," something to work for or achieve—but now I am learning something else. Rest is right here, right now—in you, in me, connected to us as we connect to Christ in us (Col. 1:27).

Real rest is being "joined with Christ."

Jesus said, "Live in me. *Make your home in me,* just as I do in you. In the same way that a branch can't bear grapes by itself but only by being joined to the vine, you can't bear fruit unless you are *joined with me*" (John 15:4 MSG).

We are not far from rest; we are close to it. Jesus invites us to be at home, at rest, in Him.

Jesus is rest.

Jesus then said, "I am the Vine, you are the branches. When you're joined with me and I with you, *the relationship is intimate and organic and the harvest is sure to be abundant.* Separated, you can't produce a thing" (v. 5 MSG).

Connected to Christ, in intimacy, we see a natural, abundant harvest.

Rest and our best ways are obtained through Christ.

"Anyone who separates from me," Jesus continued, "is dead-wood, gathered up and thrown on the bonfire. But if you make yourselves *at home with me, and my words are at home in you,* you can be sure that whatever you ask will be listened to and acted upon" (vv. 6–7 MSG).

United with the Prince of Peace, we live real peace. For instance, I am an author, a speaker, a mother, a daughter, a co-founder of a technology company, a servant, and a friend—and I've never been more at peace than I am now. Why? Because I found a "connected to Christ" way.

One name for God is *Jehovah Shalom,* which translates to, "The LORD is Peace." God is peace. The more we know Him, the more we know peace. The more we connect to Him, the more we connect to the source of peace.

The Seven Ways

Some of you may be saying, "Kelly, this all seems a bit high and lofty. A bit vague. How do we do this? How do we stay connected, united, and joined with Christ?"

I've asked these questions too. The practical *hows* can be where many of us get stuck. How do we begin taking a vague idea and boiling it down to actually working it out in our life, where the rubber meets the road?

How do we actually connect with Jesus, day-in and day-out?

How do we stay close when so much is coming at us? When people are demanding? When the world is trying to tell us what we need to do?

This is where this book comes in. Because of my many errors and wrong turns, I have discovered a good variety of those *hows*. How to stop letting the world boss you around. How to stand up for yourself and your needs. How to love authentically. How to make room for what matters most. How to inundate yourself in God's love so you can activate it in the world.

I aim to equip you with those hows and help you make what is vague practical. And I have included prayers so God's power can become your new empowerment. Also included at the end of the book are deep-dive questions to help you and your friends find rest.

I share my story—a lot. Sometimes, to protect other people, I've changed some small details, but I always maintain the heart of each story. My hope is that these become an uplifting testimony of encouragement that proves you can do this too!

You can find real rest.

Part 2 includes seven ways to help you live a lifestyle of rest. I believe restoration and renewal will be yours as you discover:

1. **The Way of Weakness:** encounter the kingdom.
2. **The Way of Humility:** sit in God's care.
3. **The Way of Forgiveness:** embrace God's compassion.
4. **The Way of Focus:** become worry-free and peace-filled.
5. **The Way of Less:** enjoy the presence of gladness.
6. **The Way of Words:** refresh your soul.
7. **The Way of Christ in Us:** be led to greater things.

Each way leads somewhere. The more you walk it, the more it gets carved. And the more it is carved, the easier it is for you to keep walking it, in both the little and the big.

These ways will help you stay with Jesus, in everything. Stay with Him on your commute. Stay with Him in the busyness. Stay with Him when you don't know what to do. Stay with Him when multiple demands come your way.

May the simplicity of Christ supersede the complexity of your world.

You and Me

First, you should know I am an ordinary girl. I am no different from you, no more special than you, and no more loved than you.

I say this because people tend to think that just because I am an author I am different, more spiritual, or somehow higher. These are all untrue. I have days when my perfectionism gets me anxious, I feel uncertain about what my future holds, or I want to control things. Ain't no one perfect. I am growing, learning, and discovering with Jesus too. At the same time, it is true that I have grown leaps and bounds in learning how to carry peace, stay with God, and live from a place of continual rest. I say all this so you know that obtaining the peace of God is just as within your reach as it is for me.

Like I said, I am pretty normal. I live on the East Coast. I have two kids I love cuddling with. I have a husband who loves to eat chicken wings and tikka masala as much as I do. I take walks to keep fit. I love voice-text messaging my friends little notes of encouragement. I have the most fun when I am outside with a coffee in hand or at home with a book on my lap. I love to brainstorm ideas for our technology business. I try to talk with God often through the day. I need God a whole lot.

In fact, I desperately need Jesus all the time. Otherwise rushing, busyness, distraction, insecurity, and mediocre junk overtake me. And I don't want to be overtaken by all that but rather overtaken by God and all the peace that comes with Him.

Maybe you feel this way too. You are yearning for more hope, more space, more room to think and thrive—but it keeps getting taken away. It feels out of reach. Like you can't grasp peace.

I felt like this for a long time. Until I resolved to realize what Jesus had *already given* me: peace.

Jesus said, "I am leaving you with a gift—peace of mind and heart. And the peace I give is a gift the world cannot give" (John 14:27).

New friend, what if the peace you search for, you already have? This book will, in many ways, help you see and seize what Christ has already given you. Expect Scripture you may have read a thousand times to move from concept to living reality.

Jesus *has already given* you peace. You will learn to connect to the Prince of Peace to live—to His peace. Rest assured, He is not holding anything back. Jesus already left it for you.

In a way, I want to take you on the journey I've adventured through, but far more quickly. This way, you won't have to circle the same mountain five hundred times. You'll get where you're going quicker than I did.

If what God has done in me is any indication of what He will do in you, be encouraged! I now feel far less obligated to say yes. I better know my needs and wants. I love others more authentically without hating myself afterward for how I "overdid" it. I allow others to take care of themselves, without the guilt and shame of thinking *I should have done more.* I take time without feeling selfish. I love my family first, rather than putting everyone else above them. I am 98 percent free of anxiety and worry. I am more loving and caring toward others than I have ever been at any point of my life. I am full of desire for Jesus, in a way where I want Him more than anything else. I am healed of an eating disorder. I am well fed, spiritually and emotionally. I am ready to travel. I am full of life. I am almost entirely free of my need to please others. I am more full of faith. I love life. I am not dependent on others to buoy my ego. I don't feel I have to perform to be loved by Jesus.

I am free to be me. I am free to be who Christ created me to be. I am free to fail. I am able to go. I am able to rest. I am able to listen. I am able to learn. I am able to change. I am able to adjust course. I am able to be patient toward myself and kind as I grow. I am able to set boundaries with foresight to preserve what matters most—as you will learn too, toward the end of the book.

I am more and more at home with Christ. It's the best thing ever! He loves me.

I believe all this will be yours too.

prayer

Jesus, I want You to meet me here. I want to live by Your heart, through Your heart, and to honor Your heart. I ask You to come into these very pages to teach me, to lead me, and to grow me. I need Your enabling, equipping, and empowering grace. I thank You that You have left me peace. I thank You that You paid such a heavy price for it. I ask You to help me live by it. I want to uncover a lifestyle of real rest. I want to know what rest in my world actually looks like. Please soften my heart so that I don't just understand these concepts in my mind but also live them and own them in my heart. I praise and thank You that You are always faithful. I trust You. I lean not on my own understanding. Please come and lead me in all Your ways. In Jesus's name. Amen.

PART 1

our unrest

ONE

our endless pursuit of more

Recently, my family moved from one state to another, and we needed new things. Because of this, I and my two chattering kids got in the car and set out to a shopping center to get some necessities: hand towels, an ironing board, and a new kitchen table.

However, the more I looked at "stuff," the more I considered how behind the times I was. It was as if every fashion had changed while I was at home tending to life. Home décor and furniture items were much lighter and whiter than they were heavy and gray—like the stuff I had at home.

I started to think about how I needed more of the *right stuff.*

Suddenly, rather than feeling at peace with inviting new friends over, I felt apprehensive. I needed to catch up with the times. I needed "more." "More" pretty. "More" like the pictures on social media. "More" in order to be welcoming. "More" to make sure I was likable.

But I knew I shouldn't spend more, so I left and clattered my clunky cart toward my car. But as I did, I quickly got lost in regretful thoughts. *I should have bought the plant. My placemats really are stained. I need a complete overhaul of my house.*

My mind was entirely lost someplace else.

Until it *wasn't.* I can't say why it happened, but somehow I just stopped walking. It was then I looked up and saw *them.* All the other people.

I wondered if perhaps, like me, they felt they had to buy "more" to feel more. More valuable? More significant? Even more, I wondered if they too were lost in their own minds. They looked lost, mechanical, on auto-pilot.

Maybe they worked Monday through Friday only to earn this day of Saturday shopping rest? Was this even rest?

I watched people finagling a picture frame into a trunk. Someone arguing about what color rug would look the best in the living room. A person with a venti-sized Starbucks Frappuccino walking and looking at a phone at the same time.

It was there, in that big store parking lot, my eyes were opened to something new: the endless pursuit of more. We feel so obligated to keep up that we get horribly tired. Tired from the more, more, more . . .

More long lines and packed parking lots.

More storing up stuff.

More appearing a certain way.

More working late to buy more things we think we need.

More anxiety because we have so little time and so much to do.

More to handle.

"More" is not confined to shopping or material things. It goes beyond that. We do more—and get more busy—to gain more appreciation or significance, or to protect ourselves.

But how is it working out for us?

Look at it from the financial angle. Approximately 80 percent of us are in debt because we are buying more.[1] And 48 million Americans are still paying off last year's Christmas bill.[2] Worry, fear, and stress are increasing. Conflicts arising in marriage. Tensions mounting.

Culture tells us that to acquire more is to be more respectable. Yet as culture ever changes, we are left ever chasing *things*. No wonder we are worn out.

I don't know about you, but in many ways I just want to throw my arms up. I'm tired of hating myself for the ways I fall behind, whether it be achieving the perfect-looking body, getting the right clothes, representing an image via my house, appearing right on social media, running after success, or winning people's approval.

Why do I work so hard for those things, anyway?

God validates me. It's culture that constantly invalidates me, telling me that I am insignificant unless I do more, buy more, or be more.

More activities with the kids so they are at the top of their class.

More Bible study so I don't feel less when around "holy" people.

More makeup so I don't have to feel bad about my looks.

More TV to rest.

More exercise lest I become the "fat mom."

More likes on social media, so I feel like I said something good.

More work, so I can get affirmation from others.

More commuting here and there, so my kids can be like other kids.

More worry that I am not measuring up.

More worth from what I do, what I buy, and what I present to others.

More. More. More.

Where are you pursuing more? How is it ruling—or ruining—your life?

You know what else I noticed in that parking lot? Not one person looked happy. Not a single one.

They looked dazed. Despondent. And bored.

Somehow, I think people in parking lots across the nation may feel the same way. Studies show Americans are the least happy we've ever been, and yet we have everything we could ever want and more.[3] For all our patterns, styles, pictures, products, solutions, makeup, and fashions galore, we kind of hate things and are classified as the most negative culture in the whole world.[4]

The endless pursuit of more is killing us; we lack rest, peace, and joy.

This was also evident to me on social media the other morning. One mom had written a post about her tiredness and weariness. I felt bad for her. The lady explained she was exhausted. I could feel her pain. I wanted to reply with something meaningful and encouraging to her soul. But do you know what nearly one-third of the comments told her to do?

"Go buy wine," one lady said. "I'll bring you three bottles."

This surprised me. Somehow, I don't think alcohol, a depressant, will lead her to more rest and recovery.

This woman wasn't looking for a party. She was looking for something more. Something more akin to soul rest: meaning, purpose, and peace. She was looking for affirmation of her worth.

Yet the world's solution is "get drunk." Hangovers don't bring peace. What culture drives us to really needs to be questioned. The world has opinions, but it is only God's ways that bring *real* joy.

A few months ago my friend Sylvia told me about her time living in Africa. What gripped her was the children. They had nothing, she said. Barely any toys. No big-screen TVs. No constant entertainment available to them at the swipe of a finger. No abundance of choices. Yet she told me, "The kids were so happy. They smiled all the time."

She went on to say that for fun they'd hit a tire rim down the road—and they loved it. They didn't need much and they had "little," yet these Liberians were the happiest group of people she ever saw.

"Little" can be extreme happiness. Immense joy.
But our "everything" exhausts us.

Catching Counterfeits

Do you know how the government identifies counterfeit money? They examine what is fake to find what's wrong. Placing a bill up against the light, they notice the embedded ribbon is missing. Aligning the bill just right, they detect the color-changing ink is not present. Using a magnifying glass, they notice that the particular USA wording is incorrect. Seeing what is wrong allows them to identify what is right—the real deal.

Wisdom discerns what is wrong to figure out what is right. What have you wrongly believed about rest?

For instance, some get to their breaking point and blow up in anger to let their family know they need a few hours off. But seeking rest this way is counterfeit. Guilt steals rest.

There are many other ways we seek and believe in counterfeit rest. Do you ever say any of the following things to yourself?

- *I can only rest after everything is accomplished.*

    It is easy to think, *I have to do more.* Yet somehow there is always more to do, and thus rest gets pushed out. Ever experienced this?
- *When I succeed, then I can be at ease.*

    There is a false idea that if we can get to a certain level, then we will have "made it" and can finally rest.

- *My happiness is conditional on others.*

  "If only they would . . ."

  "If he would change I could . . ."

  "I can't enjoy this if she is . . ."

  It can be easy to decide others need to "be some-where" so that we too can be at the point of happiness. This is false rest.

- *By doing it faster, by being a better multitasker, I can rest more quickly.*

  We can run at such a breakneck speed that we can't keep up with our own mind. When we finally do sit down, we can feel lost and disconnected from God and the peace He brings, because our mind is still running at that fast pace.

- *I failed, so I can't rest.*

  In the face of failure, it can be easy to get working on a "room for improvement" plan. *We* have to fix this—now, after all! Rest is always postponed.

- *Only when _____ happens can I _____.*

  For this person, rest is more about getting some-where than about going with God. This person consistently delays rest because there is more they have to do.

What other thoughts tend to defer your rest or deter you from it? What else do you tell yourself you need to acquire or achieve before you can rest?

31

prayer

Father, I need You, as Dad, to teach me how to rest. Will You?
In Jesus's name. Amen.

Welcome God into Your Rest

So here's what I want you to do, God helping you: take your every-day, ordinary life—your sleeping, eating, going-to-work, and walking-around life—and place it before God as an offering. Embracing what God does for you is the best thing you can do for him. Don't become so well-adjusted to your culture that you fit into it without even thinking. Instead, fix your attention on God. You'll be changed from the inside out. Readily recognize what he wants from you, and quickly respond to it. Unlike the culture around you, always drag-ging you down to its level of immaturity, God brings the best out of you, develops well-formed maturity in you. (Rom. 12:1–2 MSG)

10 Simple Ways to Welcome God into Your Rest

1. Recognize the places where the world's immaturity may lure you in.
2. Offer every little thing you do to God.
3. Ask for God's help in everything.
4. Look for what God is doing. Give thanks for it.
5. Make space to connect with God: walk, sit, listen to music, and so on.
6. Discern what God is saying through Scripture, prayer, or people.
7. Invest in the areas of your life that are most important: family, God, church, and so on. Take an inventory of where

you currently spend your time and how you want to spend it.

8. Take care of yourself: eat healthier foods, get enough sleep, and drink water.

9. Allow good friends to speak into your life.

10. Say no when distractions try to divert you.

TWO

what is your truth?

My husband, noticing my obvious irritation, asks, "Kelly, what's wrong?"

"Nothing. I'm fine," I say, complementing my words with a deep sigh and groan under my breath.

I hope shoving dishes into the pantry—loudly—makes it perfectly obvious that I'm not happy. I quicken my pace, divert my eyes from his, and figure, *He should know by now that something isn't right.*

Truly, I feel furiously flustered. I've been doing so much. I've been handling everything. I am up to my neck in things that have to be done, taking care of people who need to be loved, and I'd like a little help. He should really know all I've been dealing with. It's a lot. I need help. I can't do all this alone. I know he does his best, and he does so much, but I just need a little sympathy. A little love.

"Kelly, are you sure you are okay?"

Voice like honey, I say again, "I'm fine."

Then I start shoving things again; I wipe down the counter while violently pushing junk to one side.

I know I shouldn't be acting like this, so now I also feel horribly guilty, which compounds the negativity of my every expression. I hate how I am acting.

But I don't know what else to do.

Ever felt like this? Or acted like this?

You know you should admit you need assistance, yet you act like a jerk instead of crying out for help. You know what you should be doing, yet you act out in order to be saved.

The pressure is real. The need for help crashes down, quickly. The sense of being out of control hits its boiling point—the fact that we're powerless is too much to handle and we just . . . explode! Oh, I know how it is.

When you are handling a sick parent . . . when three kids are pulling at your hem . . . when your boss wants those five projects done by tomorrow . . . when you haven't the faintest idea how to start something . . . when people are asking you to do the impossible . . . when you know you can't hold everyone's weight, including your own . . . when your health takes a left turn . . . when you feel more than out of control . . . when you can't get a second to think.

All of it can feel so depleting and overwhelming.

But, like all the other "good women," we do what we always do: we just handle it. We pull on our big girl pants and we press on, anyway.

We don't talk about it. We put our head down. We push through. We wipe the faces. We tidy the house. We make the phone calls. We return to the doctor's office. We hug and kiss our husband. We line up tomorrow's meals. And we plop on our bed at night only to get ready to do it all over again tomorrow. Again and again and again and again and again—until we hit a combustion point.

At which point we throw up our hands, act mean to people, attack the kitchen's inanimate objects like a violent hurricane, all while calling out for a savior, who tends to be our unknowing husband or child who just got home.

- Do you ever feel like you can't handle it all?
- Do you ever hit that point of combustion?
- Do you want to escape into movies, wine, or other places?
- Do you pretend everything is okay when it isn't?
- Do you press on when there may be some things you need to address?

The Truth

Lies have never fixed anything. Nor have they ever brought a single soul rest.

I lied to myself in college. When my friends confronted me, I tried to tell myself that their words were lies. I did not have an eating disorder. Meanwhile, the truth was my body was wasting away. I was terribly cranky. I didn't want to be near anyone. The truth was as plain as day; I just couldn't admit it.

Until I saw truth for *truth*. Only when I finally admitted my truth was I able to open myself up to God's healing.

The revealing of truth is God's healing of the soul. Hiding is denying His power to save.

Some of you may want to say, "Kelly, I don't lie. I tell the truth."

To you, I say, "Really? Do you ever change what you want to say because people cannot handle it? Do you ever pretend to be okay when you are not? Do you ever press on, not paying attention to what is really going on within you?"

Lying to oneself is called *denial*. Denial is not admitting something that is true. These days, denial is rampant. Research, in fact, shows that "60 percent of people lie during a 10-minute conversation, telling approximately 2–3 lies," but just because it is prevalent doesn't make lying right or good.[1]

Dishonesty perpetuates nervousness, which leads to anxiety. Is the nervousness we hide away, live with, struggle through, and altogether hate good for us? Is it even working out for us?

Anytime we hide *our real truth* for some other variation of "truth," our soul is uneasy. Worry increases. To compound the issue, we deny what really is happening for what we think will happen. We live declaring that a horrible future is bound to hurt us. Then we feel shame.

The cycle is killing us. We say, "No, I really am not tired."

"No, I really am not angry."

"No, I really am not at my breaking point!"

But inside we feel like a wreck. I should know . . . but what about you?

38

Ask yourself: *Do I ever . . .*

- Hide my dreams under the day's duties?
- Pretend that what I want doesn't really matter?
- Reject help because requesting it makes me feel inadequate?
- Ignore the still, small voice of God when He calls me to pay attention to something?
- Rationalize what I've always done?
- Project onto others blame for what I cannot vocalize?
- Negate my feelings so as to keep some perceived "high standing" with Jesus and lie about where I am really at?

Just think: If I saw you in the grocery store and said, "How are you?" would you respond, "Fine. How about you"?

Or would you say, "Life is hard, or at least it feels that way right now. I completely lost it on my kids and feel like *that* mom. Sometimes, I feel I can't get it together"? I would likely say back to you, "You know what? Me too. I've been feeling . . ."

If you chose the latter, perhaps we'd connect. Hug. Encourage each other. Pray. And then laugh about it, right there in the store. And we'd end up with real relationship.

But we usually miss these opportunities. Instead we deny, deciding that the person would like us less *if they knew*. However, researchers have proved otherwise. They have found "self-disclosure builds trust and seeking help can boost learning.

Admitting mistakes fosters forgiveness, and confessing one's romantic feelings can lead to new relationship."[2]

Honesty is the best policy. Jesus was always honest. Jesus cried out in pain as He endured the cross. Jesus expressed grief. Jesus didn't hide His wounds. He allowed them to be seen by Thomas and others.

If Jesus showed Himself to others, why shouldn't we?

Freedom is truthfulness. The truth will set us free (John 8:32).

When we deny truth, we deny the help we need and reject God's healing. Not because of Him, but because, like Eve, we don't want to be seen by Him. We run and hide. And you can't force someone to get help when they don't want it.

For instance, try helping a sick kid take bitter medicine when he is convinced he is well. He won't take it. Why would he? But if that same kid knows he is sick? If he is coughing, struggling . . . he'll gulp down that sour stuff faster than you can say "quick."

What have you been hiding? What feels hard to admit? The fear you don't want to say? Why do you hide? Is it because you feel that you will be less?

To get to the end of ourselves—our self-preservation, our fear, our uncertainty, our abilities, our personal ideologies—is to get to the *more* of God.

You're blessed when you're at the end of your rope. With less of you there is **more of God and his rule**. (Matt. 5:3 MSG)

The kingdom of God is . . . righteousness, peace and joy in the Holy Spirit. (Rom. 14:17 NIV)

Changing Negative Patterns

We think change is bad. We would rather keep things as they are. In our mind, a current bad reality is better than a potentially worse one. We know "our bad." It's familiar. It's comfortable. So we live with it.

It is for reasons like this that a woman ends up with a man who is just like her abusive father. Or that people repeatedly find themselves in dead-end jobs they hate. Subconsciously, we repeat our same patterns, because we know them.

But I want you to understand something: new is not always bad.

There is more of God and His rule waiting for you . . . but it requires *new*. New truth. New admissions.

Think about what "newness of God" you could obtain if you simply admitted:

I am tired of endlessly pursuing more in this way.

This isn't working.

I don't like _____.

I am making mistakes in this way: _____.

I am sorry, God, that I have _____.

You may be able to say:

I have more space, time, and room to pursue what God created me to do instead.

Wow, He is teaching me patience in communication and with myself.

It is amazing that God wants to take care of me like He takes care of others.

I am okay with growing; it means I am learning and discovering.

Admitting truth to God sets us free. Remember that. It is the start of living *from* rest, rather than *for* it.

About a year ago, I found myself constantly jealous of one girl. I kept looking to see what she was doing, how she was ahead of me, and where I was falling short. I wanted what she had. I felt less than. I knew God was not okay with this, and I agreed. I could not go on living or feeling this way any longer.

So I admitted truth and told God I needed saving. I screamed out to God something like, "Deliver me from this, God! I refuse, I absolutely refuse to carry on this way." Then, for days, I set down all the million side things I was doing to go after this issue with God. I expected Him to show up.

And, after about a week, God delivered me. Fully. Remarkably. Miraculously, I no longer felt jealous of her. In fact, I felt like I wanted to help her. I could pray for her again. I loved her again.

It was done. God did it.

Often, honesty ushers in Christ's victory.

God is not afraid of truth like we are. He doesn't fear what we fear. He won't abandon us because we are negative. He is not scared off by honesty; He loves to help. And He loves to teach us from a place of truth.

When we are truthful, we learn.

In the past, from truthfulness, I've learned:

Nighttime is the best time to share with my husband how he can help me.

I can admit that I don't like shopping, nor do I like keeping up with everyone else.

I don't always find Bible time on the couch refreshing; I need to get out of the house.

I may have outgrown this friendship, but there is a great opportunity with that new girl.

I don't really need to organize the cabinets as much as I've convinced myself I do.

I defend myself to the bitter end, even though, underneath it all, I know I am wrong. Why? Because I feel ashamed of myself.

I am quick to judge others and to make assumptions based on my feelings.

What are some of your seemingly simple truths? Harder truths? What might God be trying to teach you through honesty? How might truth want to redirect you?

Truth Sets Us Free and Brings Meaning

Not too long ago, I said to a friend, "I told the Sunday school people, when they asked me, that I didn't want to help. Frankly, I am with kids nonstop and I don't want to be with more kids on Sunday. I don't feel called to it. I don't really serve at church."

A little bit of guilt snuck up on me as I said the words. *I should be doing everything I can for church. I should be showing up before the doors open—to clean them. I should be staying late like so many of the volunteers do. I should be . . .*

After I admitted my truth, she raised an eyebrow and said, "But Kelly, you do serve at church. You've done a whole bunch of teachings to the women that were so impactful."

I had? Somehow I forgot about that. Really, what I was doing for church almost seemed too easy. Too fluid. Too simple. Like I wasn't really doing anything at all.

It just felt natural. Organic. Seamless.

And now, as I came to think of it, I'd forgotten other things I was doing at church. I was also running a class on spiritual growth and the church mission. I was meeting people in need. I *was* doing more than I realized. None of it was a burden. "In fact, this is love for God: to keep his commands. And his commands *are not burdensome*" (1 John 5:3 NIV).

When we work from rest, it often feels like we're hardly working.

No matter if we are cleaning the toilets, speaking on the stage, picking up trash, or giving money, when God empowers it, it becomes easier. When God's wind is behind us, it is easy to run. Jesus said, "For my yoke is easy and my burden is light" (Matt. 11:30 NIV).

In my case, after sharing my hard-to-admit truth that I did not want to serve in childcare and that I felt I wasn't doing much, I could see that I actually *was* giving. I could enjoy my work without burdens. I found rest through admitting my truth.

Often, after we admit our truth, a friend, God, or our spouse will help us see things more clearly. They'll shed more light on our situation. This is part of the rest that is found through truth-telling.

How might you be making work more difficult than it is? How might admitting truth give you fresh wind? How might you begin to see things you hadn't before? "Open up before GOD, keep nothing back; he'll do whatever needs to be done" (Ps. 37:5 MSG).

prayer

God, I am afraid to be honest. I sometimes don't like what I see. I don't like how I look before You. I feel I should be better than I am. I should have progressed further than where I am today. I should be more holy. I feel like I may be a disappointment to You or to others. Will You help me in this place? Will You help me with the shame I feel? I want to open up to You. I want to be healed by You. I want true and deep soul-repentance. I want to do a new thing. I ask for Your grace to cover me, Your hope to renew me, and Your strength to be my strength. Guide me along my way. In Jesus's name. Amen.

How to Live Truthfully before God

1. Ask God for forgiveness and help.

2. Admit you don't know how to change.

3. Receive grace: trust God to direct you.

4. Meet Him as He prompts you to go a new way.

5. Follow and obey, immediately.

6. Give thanks (even in advance) for God's faithful work, to work change in you!

THREE

how you think

Even after we admit our truth, we may find there is a distance between where we are and where we want to be.

Often we can't figure out why we can't change. This can be one of the most frustrating parts of life. We see others with peace and think, *I want that too.* We see a lady use such a sweet voice of patience with her kids when tensions rise in the car, yet we—despite our best efforts—just blow up. Yet the more we try to change our actions, the more frustrated we become.

We can't do it.

But what holds us back is not primarily our actions but our thoughts. We think, then we act.

Sadly, many of us don't think about how we think. We take this most important sphere of life and pay no attention to it. I don't say this to chide us but to awaken us. We want God's revealing to become our healing.

Let's allow God's Word to become *our* words—owned, adopted, and executed.

Why? Because your mind has the power to radically release you to rest. To guard you from the enemy. To safekeep the seeds of peace. To change your whole life.

The Girl

I recently read the novel *Before We Were Yours* by Lisa Wingate. It had been years since I spent time just sitting with a story, letting someone else's journey become mine and partaking in a restful activity that seemed almost lavish. But this was exactly what God had for me. I started with another novel, and then found myself quickly entrenched in this book.

Quite interestingly, I noted that both were stories of orphans. I hadn't intended it to happen this way, but both conveyed deep longings of children who desired to have great parents yet found themselves living in a reality that looked nothing like family bliss. Instead of fun and peace and ample food on the table, they found themselves in squalid situations—men trying to take advantage of them, clothes that looked like rags, people saying hurtful words about who the kids were and what they did, living environments that made you wonder how they ever kept alive, and accusations that could ruin their life.

In *Before We Were Yours,* the main character, Riley (or Rill), was fending for her life in an orphanage where many kids literally lost theirs. Every day, her life and her sister's life were constantly at risk.

She was unwanted. Unloved. Treated badly. Neglected. Hurt and rejected.

Yet in spite of many devastating losses, there were also glimmers of hope. When Riley and her sister finally got adopted by an amazingly loving family, it seemed everything would be fixed. Riley and her sister were a long-awaited answer to her adoptive mother's deep longing for the kids she could never have.

But Riley would have none of it. Hurt and jaded, she couldn't receive that love. Didn't think she deserved it. Couldn't believe it. Wasn't able to accept it as real. She was only an orphan, after all. So she determined not to be part of that family. Instead, she was distant and shut out all attempts at love. How could she really be lovable after all this abandonment? After all this hurt? After everything that had happened? No way.

But once she sat down at the piano bench, something came forth that was unexpected and astounding. She could play!

Her adoptive dad, musical himself, sat down next to her. He helped her find the right keys, told her how talented she was, and said he wanted to be her friend. But Riley's trauma reared its ugly head.

All of a sudden, I'm back in the hallway at [the orphanage], in the pitch dark and Riggs [abuser] has me pinned . . . blocking the air out of me and he whispers . . . "We c-can b-b-be best friends" . . .

I get up from the piano bench, smash the keys so that a handful play at once. The noise mixes with the sound of my shoes clattering against the floor. I don't stop running until I'm upstairs curled in the bottom of my closet with my feet braced on the door so no one else can get in.[1]

Riley, about to receive everything, allowed her mind to tell her it would be nothing good. We often do the same. We believe the past will repeat. We create a self-fulfilling prophecy. We reject the love trying to save us.

Our Living Reality

Often, the past becomes our living reality. We may not say it, but we remember the small offenses, the rejection, the hurt, the way we trusted and can't again. We think, *It'll happen again. I must not be lovable. God couldn't really love me that much. I'll always be hurt.*

We remember what happened as a kid or what a parent said, how a boyfriend treated us or how things played out. We remember how we were disappointed and how things never shaped up as we wanted. Perhaps God wants us hurt this way. We don't know. Either way, many of us repeatedly live the unrest of yesterday. Believing it will just happen again.

So, what happened *keeps* happening. We live like orphans. Afraid. Constantly protecting. Dodging bullets. Ducking and covering. Manipulating people's responses.

We think, *People must want something from me. I don't believe I could ever be wanted like this.* Love becomes conditional. If someone gives, there are strings attached. We'll need to pay them back. We might be punished. We have to act good to stay safe.

Do you have an orphan mindset? Ask yourself:

- Do I feel like damaged goods?
- Do I feel neglected, abandoned, or unwanted? Not pretty enough, smart enough, or good enough?
- Do I love from a distance, not really entering in because I fear rejection?
- Do I live in a protective stance, figuring people are against me?
- Do I work harder to make up for the deep sense that I am not enough?
- Do I try to act "less than" sometimes so I don't draw too much attention to myself?
- Has love eluded me?
- Do I feel cheated by people?

I know when I am falling into this mentality because I begin fending for myself. I think no one is "for me." I have to do it myself if I want it done right. I can't trust people. I don't have enough time or money. I feel isolated and alone. I develop action plans. I feel unsure and insecure.

For instance, a few weeks ago I told my husband, "I really need to crucify this repetitive behavior. . . . I need to figure this out and fix it, once and for all!"

He responded, "Kelly, do you even realize what you are saying? Think about the ramifications of you 'crucifying it' for a second."

51

I could see where he was coming from . . . I was acting as if crucifixion work was my work . . . as if I had the power to get a hammer to nail it out . . . as if that work hadn't already been done by Jesus.

Jesus was crucified. I am resurrected as a new creation. And through the Holy Spirit, I walk in the newness of life, which is His life. There is no second crucifixion needed, where I get beaten up, where I hate myself to fix myself, where I do a whole bunch of work to get better.

Arrogance is hidden right below false humility. As if I could add more to the work Jesus Christ did on the cross, already! *God, forgive me.*

We know that our old sinful selves were crucified with Christ **so that sin might lose its power** in our lives. We are no longer slaves to sin. (Rom. 6:6)

We are now children of God.

I cannot redo the work of Jesus, taking on things He already accomplished. I can't save my kids or my husband. Only Jesus is Savior and Sovereign. I can't handle everything, as if it is up to me. These thoughts can look like servant-righteousness, but they are more about me and my goals, my plans and my strategies.

How are you acting like an orphan when in reality you've been adopted as a child?

Do you do more to get more? Try harder to be more loved? Apologize often? Hide your weaknesses so you don't get punished? Muster up self-power to make sure you are okay? Take credit so you rise to the top of the pack? Cover up your feelings that you figure don't really matter anyway?

God adopted you. And He still wants you.

Work Days

When I was young, I liked work days with my dad. He would bring me to his office, which was in a skyscraper. There, feeling miles above the rushing cars and pedestrians, I felt on top of the world looking out at all the mini-cars below. My dad would show me things. He was a stockbroker. He'd set me on his lap, and I'd look at charts.

"It is the teacup you want to keep your eye out for," he said. "When you see the handle and the cup, you know the market is going to break. It is then you want to invest." Of course, at that point in my life his words were gibberish to me, but it didn't much matter. He was showing me the best of what he had. He was giving me access to his world, even though I was young. None of it mattered; I just liked being on his lap, close to him.

Dad had it all. The keys to the elevator that lifted me up sky-high to a world of business opportunity. The "in" to the office doors closed to the outside world. Dad revealed things to me in that office that only a daughter would get to know. He gave me the inside scoop. He pulled me close. He gave me his best. He loved me, despite the calls, needs, and busyness outside his glass-walled fishbowl. This is what good dads do.

But notice here: I had to be willing to travel with him. If I didn't trust him, believe that he really was my dad . . .

53

if I didn't think he really cared, I would not have followed him up to the office. I would have stayed home, bowed out, told him, "I don't want to go today." And I would have missed out.

When we know we belong to God, that we are part of His family, and that we are wanted (Eph. 1:4–5), we follow Him. We don't fight, worry, postulate, or stir up unrest; we lean into love. We sit on His lap. We learn.

Because I knew my dad loved me, wanted me, and cared for me and that I belonged to him, I knew he would not abandon me or give me away in that building. I knew he would take me where I needed to go. I didn't have to pull away or hide until he was gone.

Some of us need to know that God is a good Father. I mean this. You need to accept, deep down, that God *really*, truly, and completely has adopted you. Wants you. You absolutely belong in His family. You are undoubtedly called holy and blameless. He has good things for you.

God's banner over you is love. One of God's names is *Jehovah Nissi*, which means, "The LORD is my banner." As a child of God, there is an unmistakable and unbreakable banner of love over you. This love welcomes you to His banqueting table.

You are not abandoned; you are wanted. Wholly and forevermore. What saving work Jesus has done *is* done.

Consider: If my dad, an earthly man, gave me good gifts and wisdom, how much more does your heavenly Daddy give you good gifts (Matt. 7:11)? Your Daddy provides, protects, and pays attention to you.

You Are Loved

Close your eyes and think about what the best dads do for beloved daughters. They fight for them. They teach them. They show them. They lead them. They bring them nice things. They give to them. They, at all costs, protect.

If "God did not send his Son into the world to condemn the world, but to save the world through him" (John 3:17 NIV), why would He abandon you now?

God is one hundred million times better than even the best human father, and countless miles different from the worst dad. Never allow trauma and drama to speak over God. God has good for you. Even in the bad, there is good. God is "abounding in love and faithfulness" (Exod. 34:6 NIV).

Sometimes, when I am not sure about how God feels toward me, I think about parenting. If my learning-to-talk kid couldn't get his words out, would I yell at him? Would I scream, "Just say it already!"? Or would I just encourage him . . . and be patient?

When I stop and think practically about what good parents do, this helps me when I feel God might be angry, upset, or distant. How might you need to look through a "good parent" lens?

Perceptions, assumptions, or convictions about others are not always reality. I've had to learn this the hard way. We should think the best of others. At the same time, we must be honest about our personal needs. This is not the same as using a victim mindset to get benefits such as sympathy or compassion. We can too easily think, *People never look out for me. I always get hurt. I am always left behind. A victim needs care.*

Choose to state your needs rather than lick your wounds. We remain incapacitated when we rely on others, on outcomes, or on results to save us. We stunt our progress.

- Where have your hurts defined who God is to you and how He relates to you?
- Where have you permitted circumstances or people to lessen God's care?
- How are triggers or instinctive responses distancing you from God's love? Or from getting needed help?

Orphans live dependent on conditions; children of God live dependent on God's unconditional love. A child of God rests in the position of *loved.* This always-secure positional love cannot be removed, tainted, or taken away. Do you know, beyond a shadow of a doubt, that you are positioned in God's always-there love? You are hidden in Christ, you are God's possession, you are wanted, you are chosen, you are adopted. More than conditional love, positional love is *rest.*

Positional love says, "My Daddy is the manager, owner, and orchestrator of the world. He has 'glorious, unlimited resources' (Eph. 3:16) available at His right hand. He tells me I am His masterpiece. He wants to help me. He hears me when I call. He loves me—always. He is ready to help. He is watching. He is not looking to condemn me. He has good plans laid out for me."

Positional love aims to stay under God's lordship and does not stray left or right, or out into sin, worry, or fear.

Positional love expects, hopes, trusts, and believes—*big*. It lies down under an ever-flowing waterfall of God's unending love. It keeps on receiving all He has.

> May He grant you out of the riches of His glory, to be strength-ened and spiritually energized with power through His Spirit in your inner self, [indwelling your innermost being and per-sonality], so that Christ may dwell in your hearts through your faith. And may you, having been [deeply] rooted and [securely] grounded in love, be fully capable of comprehend-ing with all the saints (God's people) the width and length and height and depth of His love [fully experiencing that amazing, endless love]; and [that you may come] to know [practically, through personal experience] the love of Christ which far surpasses [mere] knowledge [without experience], that you may be filled up [throughout your being] to all the fullness of God [so that you may have the richest experience of God's presence in your lives, completely filled and flooded with God Himself]. (vv. 16–19 AMP)

prayer

Father God, I want to know You as a good Father. I want to know Your care. I want to uncover Your heart. I may not have experienced this kind of love before, but will You make it known to me? I may not have felt that anyone cared much, but will You care for me? I want to know the depths and lengths of Your love. I want to rest in Your arms. I want to discover how much You take care of me. In Jesus's name. Amen.

How to Habitually Rest in God's Love

1. Know who you are in Christ and what Christ thinks of you (see chapter 13).
2. Agree that it is "for freedom that Christ has set you free" (Gal. 5:1 NIV). Decide you will walk in it.
3. Ask God for help.
4. Fill your mind with prayer and recite God's Word. The more you are filled with God's thoughts, the less you will be filled with thoughts of insecurity.
5. When you feel "less than" or that you have to be "more than," ask Him what He thinks of you. Search Scripture to understand God's heart toward you.

FOUR

recovering prayer

Rest is having a Dad who looks out for you. You don't have to look over your shoulder all the time. And once you really believe you are loved, you can do one thing that can truly change your life. . . .

You can start praying—or start praying again.

Many of us have stopped. Or if we do pray, it is a quick two-minute check-in before dinner or right before bed. It is rote. It is monotone and without much belief behind it. Often it is words spoken without heart. Our mind may not even be much aware of what our mouth is saying. It is not that we don't want to pray—actually, we know we *should* pray—but we haven't seen much happen through prayer. So we become distant to prayer. It seems like something God wants from us rather than something that is a benefit to us.

And so, we have no outlet. We stuff all our frustrations. We feel hopeless. Aimless. Lost. Stuck. We have to figure things out on our own.

This is a gargantuan issue, because when prayer ceases, nervousness increases. Prayerlessness is a silent beast. It is the antithesis of rest.

It is why we often find ourselves burned out or completely overwhelmed.

God has better things to deal with, we figure. Other people have more issues than we do. World hunger. Terrorism. Politics. What right do we have to need His help when so many others are in need? When things are so horrible? Our stuff is small. We should be "over it" already. Or so we tell ourselves.

But I wonder what would happen if we went five thousand levels deeper? Might we admit that we are a little upset with God? That we asked Him for stuff He didn't give? That we've been asking for years to get out of this situation, but we're still waiting? That we are tired and we expected more from Him?

Now we feel stuck. How does one go about fixing the chaos of marriage issues, relational turmoil, lost kids, or financial ruin all by themselves? It all feels like too much.

Our lack of prayer leads to an excess of worry.

- -

My husband and I were in this place recently. A prayer crisis, if you will. It is not that we didn't want to pray; we just hadn't seen God answer *very important* prayers. Ones we thought were sure to happen. Ones that seemed good. Ones that we thought were bound to come through. Those things? They went kaput. They fell flat. So we just lobbed up halfhearted words to Jesus without having our whole heart behind them. We prayed full of doubt.

[Jesus said,] "Truly I tell you, if anyone says to this mountain, 'Go, throw yourself into the sea,' and does not doubt in their heart but believes that what they say will happen, it will be done for them. Therefore I tell you, whatever you ask for in prayer, believe that you have received it, and it will be yours." (Mark 11:23–24 NIV)

This passage seems to say, "Believe it and immediately see it. Believe greatly! Bold! Big!"

But what about my prayers? What happened to them? After being confronted with this verse in my Bible, I was confused. Why didn't what I prayed for happen? I believed. Why did I get emotionally hurt? Why was I crushed for months with discouragement? *I really thought that God would have . . . I really thought that God should have . . .*

Have you ever been there? Asking, "Why, God, why?" Wondering how God forgot you, and feeling left behind and neglected in your time of need?

I relate. I know God is good, I know He has a good plan. But sometimes it is just *hard.*

On the flip side, I know prayer works. I've seen prayer so powerful it moves mountains. I have seen people evangelized and saved through prayer. I have seen people physically healed because a prayer warrior believed. I have seen someone become less afraid to speak to large groups because of prayer. I have seen God touch a stranger's heart, both healing it and leading them to Jesus. I have seen someone let go of trauma that kept them victimized for years. I have seen depression immediately removed from someone's countenance and life.

Prayer works.

There have been many times my mind has said, *This is mentally impossible. Nope. No way.* But prayer worked. God answered.

So, *how much* do I believe in God to answer my prayers?

Let's look at that passage from Mark again, in the Amplified version. I think it will give you greater clarity as to the meaning of the biblical words.

Jesus replied, "Have faith in God [constantly]. I assure you and most solemnly say to you, whoever says to this mountain, 'Be lifted up and thrown into the sea!' and **does not doubt in his heart [in God's unlimited power], but believes that what he says is going to take place**, it will be done for him [in accordance with God's will]. For this reason I am telling you, whatever things you ask for in prayer [in accordance with God's will], believe [with confident trust] that you have received them, and they will be given to you." (11:22–24 AMP)

Here is how I boil this down:

My job is confident, unwavering asking.

God's job is accomplishing His will.

When I believe and don't see, His ultimate will is better than my immediate request. His goodness is superseding my conception of it.

How many of us thought an old boyfriend was "good" for us? Yet now we can look back and say, "Thank You, God, for saving me from that one." It's like that.

Retrospect is clarity. What God doesn't do is *best* for us. And the many others who may be involved.

At the same time, we must be careful about attributing evil to God's will. Is rape God's will? Is drug addiction God's will? We must also be careful in discerning what is and is not God's will (see Rom. 12:2). There is also an enemy at work in this world. Just remember that God is good—always. Set your faith on that. He is far better than even our best description of *good* could possibly be.

God is good. God does have good for us. In this, we can

confidently ask (going all in),

abandon ourselves to His best plan,

believe in His exceedingly abundantly more, and

leave all the results to Him.

But, Kelly . . .

Inarguably, some of you are now saying, "In theory, that sounds good, but still . . . I really don't understand why *my prayer* didn't work."

Maybe you were praying for someone to come to salvation. We know that this is God's will (1 Tim. 2:4). Or maybe you were praying for a reconciled marriage. Again, we know God's will *for* marriage. But you haven't seen it work out.

And your *not seeing* is preventing *your believing.*

It's as if you know in your mind you should believe, but you can't actually bring your heart to believe anymore. So you halt the power of God at work through prayer. You give up.

Now you overwork in the places where God *should have* worked. You take over the areas God does not seem to be tackling.

What do you do if you've landed yourself here, in the place of halfhearted prayers?

Sometimes you have to get more practical with fighting the good fight. I've found I can return to rest, sometimes, by creating counterarguments. In fact, I have a bunch of mini-notecards on spiritual topics that I keep in my jewelry box. They are the Scripture-centered reasons why I believe what I do. When the enemy attacks me on something, I pull out my cards to remind me why I do what I do and believe what I believe. In the same spirit, let's look at some counterarguments as to reasons why your prayers, at times, might be delayed or why they appear to be unanswered.

My hope is that, by doing this, God will resurrect your prayer life so that His miraculous work will supersede your hard work. Then, you will do less and God will do more. His work is a million times more effective and longer lasting than yours.

If I had a notecard about "Why doesn't God always answer prayers on my timeline?" I might have written these six things on it.

1. God is growing things.

It is through tearing that muscles grow stronger. Sometimes our heart tears a bit as we wait. This is not bad. We learn the re-surrendering process. In this, we grow strong. Strong people help others grow stronger.

2. God desires to perfectly display His glory.

Jesus waited four days to visit sick Lazarus. Lazarus ended up dying and was buried before Jesus even got there. Why would anyone delay when there is a deathly ill person in need?

Jesus said, "This sickness will not end in death. No, *it is for God's glory* so that God's Son may be glorified through it" (John 11:4 NIV).

Sometimes, there is a greater glory to the story.

3. God is teaching us in testing.

"Although he was a son, [Jesus] learned obedience through what he suffered" (Heb. 5:8 ESV). I have a son. I look out for him. So much so that if he leaves his lunchbox at home, I may not bring it to him before lunch. Is that because I don't love him? No. It is because I do. I want him to learn how to stay full for the long run, rather than attending to his immediate, short-term hunger. Sometimes, there is a greater lesson in the works.

If Jesus learned obedience through suffering, how much more does God use our suffering for good? As my friend Julie says, "Our God is not a wasteful God."

4. God is protecting us.

Not too long ago, we left our car in a city center parking lot only to return and find a huge dent in the front right fender. When I saw it, my heart sank a bit. It was frustrating. A few weeks later, we went to a mall. When we walked back to the car, there was another football-sized dent, this time on the back right bumper of the car. *Grr . . . again? What is going on?* A few weeks later, my husband walked into the house after an outing with the kids and said, "I have some bad news for you, Kelly."

What happened now?

Someone slammed into the left rear side of the car. A baseball-sized hole now lived on my back bumper. I still drive the car around like this, with three sides wrecked.

And for a good while I didn't feel happy about it. *Why, God? What is going on?* I started to whine and opine a bit to my husband. "I don't understand why all this happened to us. Why didn't God protect us from all this? And now we have to pay all this money to get the car fixed."

It didn't end there. Until my husband turned to me, somewhere in the middle of my pity party, and said something like, "Kelly, you have this all wrong. What you see as God's lack of protection actually *is* God's protection. No one is in the hospital."

What I saw as destruction was likely God's protection. I stopped, asked God for forgiveness for my complaints, and thanked Him for all the unseen times He has protected me. I don't believe God set out to ruin my car, but He certainly has watched over me countless times.

It is all how we look at things.

5. God gives mini-keys, often, before the master key.

How many of us know that God uses the little to prepare us for what He considers big?

> Whoever can be trusted with very little can also be trusted with much, and whoever is dishonest with very little will also be dishonest with much. (Luke 16:10 NIV)

For instance, with that not-yet-fixed dented car I learned fearlessness as I drove it to my kids' school while all the other parents drove in with carwash-shiny perfect cars. I learned patience and nonjudgment when I saw other people driving clunkers. I learned how to teach my kids optimism when we kept on seeing dents and dings. Attitude matters more than a perfect-looking car, I realized.

6. God is training and conditioning us so that we are ready.

Consider: you don't throw a toddler in the pool before he or she is ready to swim. But the day that you do? Boy, do you celebrate. There is a preparation time, before launching time.

In the meantime, we should remember:

God's will is "good and pleasing and perfect" (Rom. 12:2).
God's will for every outcome in your life is good.
God's intent for every situation you face is pleasing.
God's design for every good thing you pray is perfect.

"Let us not become weary in doing good, for *at the proper time* we will reap a harvest if we do not give up" (Gal. 6:9 NIV).

The Persistent Lady

We don't have to be lackadaisical about our prayers. The Bible says, "Be strong in the Lord and in his mighty power" (Eph. 6:10). This verse does not say, "Resign yourself to whatever God may do," or "Understand that God will have His way anyway, so do nothing," or "Be weak, because you're just a sinner—how could you make a difference?"

This verse gives us no leeway to change nothing or to just exist. Instead, it tells us we have power to shift things. Your unrest, unsettledness, exhaustion, disillusionment, complacency, inability to make life or career changes—you can, through prayer, impact these things. "The prayer of a righteous person is powerful and effective" (James 5:16 NIV). Prayer is a power position; it effects change.

Jesus also highlighted this to His disciples. One day, "Jesus told them a story showing that it was necessary for them to pray consistently and never quit" (Luke 18:1 MSG). Essentially this story was about a woman who never quit asking for justice until she got it. Sure, she heard no at first. But she kept on asking.

Point being: do not give up.

God wants us to keep asking. Jesus once prayed for a blind man, but even after He prayed, this man's vision was still hazy. So Jesus prayed a second time. Then the man saw clearly. If Jesus asked more than once, how much more do we need to ask multiple times? Don't just resign yourself to "God's will" before you've even begun praying.

Instead, "Pray in the Spirit at all times and on every occasion" (Eph. 6:18). Why? Because you have the ability to stop the enemy, the devil, from taking ground in your life. "Hold up the shield of faith to stop the fiery arrows of the devil" (v. 16).

When you hold him back, seize God's ground! Believe in a parting of waters, a breaking of the offending army, or a healing of epic proportions.

Miracles originate through prayer. Miracles recover rest.

Do you see the power Christ has afforded you through prayer yet? This is not even to speak of the ways the armor of God, described in Ephesians 6:13–17, can divert spiritual attacks as they pertain to mental unrest, turmoil, and unsettled, worry-filled thoughts.

Remind yourself, *No, I am not ruined. I am saved, eternally and always and forever, because of Jesus. It is finished. I praise and thank You for this, Jesus. I put on the "peace of the good news" and "salvation like a helmet."*

Many times unsettling attacks are over the second you pray, and the victory is only one "Amen" away! Don't give up.

Stepping It Up on the Prayer Front

Step it up on the prayer front.

Imagine this: there is a war being fought. There is an enemy approaching your camp. The General is certainly still in command-position, on the high hill, reigning. He may not be right next to you, but He has not left you ill-equipped. He has given you the Holy Spirit, who is in your tent. Jesus said, "It is for your good that I am going away. Unless I go away, the Advocate will not come to you; but if I go, I will send him to you" (John 16:7 NIV).

Even though it looks like you are by yourself, things are not as they appear. The Commander, your Advocate and Counselor, the Holy Spirit, is ready to help you win this battle. This is why you must "pray in the Spirit at all times" (Eph. 6:18). Your prayer will "stop the fiery arrows." Your prayer will help you "stand firm against [evil] strategies" (v. 11). You have the blueprint. The Commander knows the battlefield.

The Spirit can fight spiritual things better than you can, and the Spirit Himself prays for you (Rom. 8:26). And because of the Spirit—even when the battle looks rough and the decks are stacked against you—you find yourself knowing and going with hope, peace, and joy.

The battle is being fought for you, no matter what it looks like on the battlefield (see Exod. 14:14).

The Holy Spirit is your Advocate. Peace is knowing this (John 14:26).

You have what you need to win the war. You have the best Advocate inside you, the One Jesus left you, to guide and to help. You are filled. You are not on defense but on offense.

Reclaim the rest Christ won for you; take it back again through prayer. Prayer is not continual begging; it is proclaiming truth. It is asking. It is seeking God. It is watching what He is doing. It is believing again. It is uncovering God's plan. It is a posture of power, not defeat. Start today.

Start by praying these verses over your life:

May the God of hope fill [me] with all joy and peace in believing, so that by the power of the Holy Spirit [I] may abound in hope. (Rom. 15:13 ESV)

[Thank You, God, that Jesus has] given [me] authority to trample on snakes and scorpions and to overcome all the power of the enemy; [and] nothing will harm [me]. (Luke 10:19)

Prayer is a pinnacle-point of rest. Pray like you know God will do it, and release the results to His perfect, good, and pleasing plan for your life. Above all, don't quit.

prayer

Father God, thank You that freedom is saying "Your will be done." You have a good plan. Thank You also that You say

Jesus has left me peace. Peace is deciding that what You most want I do too. In this, and with this, I can thank You for every "no," because each and every one is actually a better "yes." Truly, God, Your ways, plans, and intentions are higher, better, and more perfect than anything I could think up on my own. Your course of action is good. I praise You for what You are doing, orchestrating, forming, and planning. Give me strength to wait on You, to lean on You, and to trust in You. Give me wisdom about when to keep asking and when to start addressing the demonic things coming against me. Give me discernment for my moves and wisdom in the way I walk. May dread, discouragement, and disillusionment stay far from me. And may I continually have eyes to see what You're giving rather than taking from me. May hope flood my every prayer, and may I believe You for the big things. Grant me the joy of seeing Your hand in every prayer, and when You show up grant me the humility to give all glory and honor to You. In Jesus's name. Amen.

Seven Power Prayers

Paul was a prayer warrior. In many of his letters to the churches, he prayed. I have found so much encouragement and life in praying the words of the Bible over my life. And when I pray Paul's prayers, I feel even more uplifted. Lighter.

Here are seven power prayers as summed up through Paul's words.

1. **"God, I thank You for others. Even when I can't under-stand them, I want to love them. Help me to be a uniter, not a divider."** (Phil. 1:3–6; Rom. 1:8–10; Eph. 1:15; Col. 1:9–10; 2 Thess. 1:3)

2. **"God, fill me with Your goodness. Through this, may Your name be glorified."** (Rom. 12:2; Phil. 4:6–7; Eph. 2:14–23; 2 Thess. 3:16)

3. **"May the power of Jesus Christ continually fill me with joy, grace, peace, and hope, in believing, by the power of the Holy Spirit."** (Rom. 15:13; 1 Cor. 16:23; Col. 1:9–14).

4. **"May my heart continually pursue You. May I hear, under-stand, and uncover all You have to say to me through Your Word and in prayer. Give me the words and wisdom I so desperately need."** (Rom. 15:30–33; Col. 4:2–4; Eph. 6:19–20)

5. **"God, You are the fullness of all I desire, want, hope for, and need. Come and be my everything."** (2 Cor. 1:3–7; Eph. 1:3)

6. **"I lack no good thing, Father God. Thank You for every-thing."** (1 Cor. 1:4–9; 2 Cor. 2:14–16; 9:12–15; Phil. 4:6–7)

7. **"Father, mold me, make me, and fashion me into Your likeness. May I not hate the process but delight in the journey of doing it with You. Give me grace."** (Phil. 1:9–11; 4:23; 2 Cor. 13:7–9; 1 Thess. 5:23–24; Titus 3:15)

PART 2

the seven ways

TO COME AWAY

As we've come to see, many of us have a pattern of lying, hiding, or denying how overwhelmed we actually feel. Many of us have pursued a life of "more"—more stuff, more success, more goods, more hard work—at the expense of less time to connect with what matters most, God and His peace. Many of us are praying less and are overworked.

At this point, we likely *feel* the weight of the loads we are carrying. We now recognize how much things aren't working— how deeply we've been hurt by our own load-carrying. How there *has to be* something more.

This is a fantastic starting point.

If you see no need to change, you never will change. If you don't believe there is light at the end of your tunnel, you'll give up in dark-defeat.

Jesus speaks of the light available to folk like you and me.

Are you tired? Worn out? Burned out on religion? Come to me. Get away with me and you'll recover your life. I'll show you how to take a real rest. Walk with me and work with me—watch how I do it. Learn the unforced rhythms of grace. I won't lay anything heavy or ill-fitting on you. Keep company with me and you'll learn to live freely and lightly. (Matt. 11:28–30 MSG)

Come. Get away. Doesn't this sound nice?

God is saying to us:

Come away with Me.
You'll recover.
I'll show you.
Walk and work with Me.
Watch how I do it.

What God is about to do is more than what we have done. He invites us somewhere new.

We are about to enter into a deeper place of rest. A more profound place of recovery. Our own sort of promised land. An actual destination to which God wants to take us.

If I were to paint it as a picture, it would look like the front cover of this book: trees, a stream—a place where I can lie down. It is me lying on a blanket looking up at the clouds, seeing what God is doing; it is a space for me to think; it is hope rising; it is God teaching me; it is wonder, as I marvel at what God has done; it is room to remember; it is hope and it is life.

What I think is just marvelous about this picture is I don't have to escape my present world to enter it; it is available to me *now*—and to you too. It is available to us as we learn the "unforced rhythms of grace." Even in the crazy bustle of the day, with a million people asking us a million things, we can still meet God. With text messages galore coming in a mile a minute, we can still find our minds operating from this place. We don't even have to "demand it" of our self. "Unforced" means just that: we don't force it. Nor does it mean that God demands we do it right now. It comes naturally.

Can you imagine this at work in your life?

God calls us; we come.

God shows us things; we make sure we're positioned to see.

God takes us somewhere; we walk along with Him.

God has some things for us to do; we work.

God knows we need direction; we watch Him and He shows us how to do it.

This is what the seven ways are all about: coming away. Each way is meant to foster greater trust as we follow His leading. Some of the ways remove the barriers of fear. Others bring us low. Some give us eyes to see things we've never seen before. But all are meant to allow our heart to go away somewhere greater with God . . . somewhere that looks like *rest.*

These ways will lift us like a kite positioned just right. God's nearness, His closeness, and His heartbeat should take us to new plains of rest as we learn them.

1. **The Way of Weakness:** encounter the kingdom.
2. **The Way of Humility:** sit in God's care.
3. **The Way of Forgiveness:** embrace God's compassion.
4. **The Way of Focus:** become worry-free and peace-filled.
5. **The Way of Less:** enjoy the presence of gladness.
6. **The Way of Words:** refresh your soul.
7. **The Way of Christ in Us:** be led to greater things.

As God goes, so will we. As He lives, so will we. I believe Christ will get all up into our patterns, our habits, and our mindsets. And rest will follow.

Once His Word and truth work their way to our insides, everything on the outside gets worked out.

You're blessed when you get your inside world—your mind and heart—put right. Then you can see God in the outside world. (Matt. 5:8 MSG)

The seven ways should light your insides with a renewed passion for God, so much so that outside things will naturally, seamlessly, and organically fall into their rightful places.

Come away with God a little bit . . .

FIVE

the way of weakness

ENCOUNTER THE KINGDOM

Recently, a church-girlfriend said to me, "Kelly, all the gals and I miss coming to your house. It's the only place we can *be real*."

I didn't know what to say. I had set up a few mornings as spiritual spa days of sorts. I'd tried to make my home an open place to be honest about our real and present difficulties. A meeting place to experience the love and healing of our good Father.

Some days we laughed. Others we got silly. One day, I remember, at least one of us literally screamed out to God. Many times we cried. And on occasion we danced fun dances. But no matter what, front and center was encouragement for each other, because times can get tough. Those days were good.

Really good. Praying and listening, seeking and finding, holding hands and journeying in together, without any judgment, we found true refreshment of mind even more than body.

This is not even to speak of all the amazing food, pretty flowers, and scented candles that surrounded us. We breathed deep and got to go somewhere different—pretty much to that vision of a deeper place of rest. To an unforced rhythm. To easy—or easier, at least.

But to hear this woman say that a meeting at my house once every three months was the only place she could be real? Oh my; this concerned me deeply.

Because she was right: almost nowhere do we have the freedom to be real. To be really us. To be our quirky selves. Many of us don't even know what we like anymore. Or who we really are. Or what it is to be really funny, really sad, really happy, or really needy. We feel embarrassed to be desperate for God. We feel stupid if others know how much we are really abandoned to God.

We cannot be at rest with who God created us to be.

Why is this?

The more I think about it, the more I'm aware of the shame we feel when we are real. *I can't be too much . . . can't come off too . . . can't overdo it . . . can't seem too spiritual . . . can't want to love God that much, or others may think I am one of those people. . . .*

It's as if we hear our childhood yelling at us.

Buck up, sissy! Pull yourself together, already.
Clean up your act. You know better than this.

Don't be selfish.

Don't look weak—whatever you do, don't do that!

Don't overdo it.

Don't do what everyone else is not *doing.*

Don't be overly excited. Certainly do not cry.

Don't be on fire for God.

Don't go outside the mold.

Don't make yourself look vulnerable, or you'll feel ashamed of yourself.

Shame is, according to Merriam-Webster, "a painful emotion caused by consciousness of guilt, shortcoming, or impropriety."[1] It is the idea that everyone is about to laugh at you.

Like they did when I took a risk as a preteen and invited that boy to dance. He said no—and everyone was watching. Or when, in elementary school, I asked a group of girls to play but ended up sitting on the curb by myself, alone. Or when I found a new friend only to hear her other friend say, "Don't be friends with her. She's . . ." Eventually, I changed schools.

I hated myself just a little bit more every time something else like this happened, wondering, *Why can't I be better than me?* For a long time, I lived my life continually on edge, trying to be *more* to make up for how I felt like *less.*

Many of us feel this way. We deeply fear there is something wrong with us, so we determine our weakness must remain hidden. The more we fear who we are, the more we are controlled by constant nagging feelings of shame.

Inner voices demand things of us. *Stop crying, already. Don't be dense. Stop acting like a baby. Don't be selfish. You're a burden. Shame on you.*

So, we start apologizing to others. "I am sorry I am burdening you with this." "I am sorry if this is weighing you down." "I am sorry if I am coming off too strong." "I am sorry if I seem too _____." "I am sorry, you must really think I am a horrible mom." "I am sorry, I must really appear to be _____."

We often apologize to please people and excuse away the guilt that we're "a burden."

This heightens social anxiety and worry. Recent research reports that 57 percent of women are feeling increasingly anxious and worried. About 65 percent of people between ages fifteen and forty-nine reported stress, and 51 percent reported worry.[2]

Hiding weakness spikes emotional unrest.

It's hard to have peace when you can't be weak. When you constantly have to be aware of yourself and how you are "coming off." When your mind has already convinced you that you are bad.

How do these things tire you out? How might your mind be in overdrive?

Imperfection

I am horribly impatient when people take forever to do things . . . I gaze off sometimes, daydreaming, when my husband is sharing important things . . . I pay no attention to sending thank-you cards . . . I have closets that look like a bomb exploded in them.

It took me half my marriage to realize: I have weaknesses. More recently, I almost lost a super amazing friend because of one. It all started when she made a small recommendation regarding something I should do, and I got all sensitive about it. Rather than receiving it as a simple recommendation, I blew it up into a huge proclamation of my lack. *She doesn't think I am good at this. She doesn't respect me. She doesn't value me. I must not have done a good job.*

Before I knew it, I was offended. Then I became furious. I then determined in my mind that she couldn't be trusted, she was taking advantage of me, she was not being clear about her motives, and . . .

I left her a horrid voice memo detailing all the ways that she was wrong, wrong, wrong!

Lo and behold, a few weeks later, after we actually talked, I realized *I* was horribly wrong. Head down and feeling very much like an idiot, I had to come to terms with myself. I'd blown the whole situation out of proportion by putting words in her mouth she didn't speak and outlining motives she never had.

This was not an isolated incident, either. I'm horrible. Convicted, I faced my weaknesses: *I personalize things. I make things about myself.*

There it was. I was looking at my dark secret; it was fat and it was ugly.

Ever felt this way about your weaknesses? About yourself? Ever wanted to hide your weight, your looks, your attitude,

your mistakes, your house, your car, your lack thereof, your
. . . whatever?

God brought me down about four levels that day, but some
peace came from it. I learned:

My weakness tells my friends it is okay when they feel
weak too.

People's strengths and gifts can help me see beyond my
weakness.

My sharing honors people; it shows I trust them.

I don't have to hate my weaknesses.

We all have weaknesses.

Even biblical giants had astronomical weaknesses. For
example, Paul said he was the chief sinner (1 Tim. 1:15).
Peter denied Jesus—more than once (Mark 14:66–72).
Thomas doubted Jesus's return after His resurrection (John
20:25).

No person is above weakness—but the Pharisees thought
they were. Thinking they knew it all, they judged Jesus. They
critiqued. They accused. Acting above it all, they declared
they needed no help.

I'm sure Jesus may have, at times, felt like running from
them, but He never ran from the weak. Those who were open
to His help got it. Think of who Jesus was drawn to: the pros-
titutes, the tax collectors, the insane, the criminals, the sick, the
blind beggars, the lepers, the traitors, the lame, the doubting,
the adulterers. He said, "I have come to call *not those who think*

they are righteous, but *those who know they are sinners* and need to repent" (Luke 5:32).

Jesus saves those in need. Admitting you are weak creates room for Him to be strong. Admitting sin gives room for healing. Admitting you need saving clears the way for it.

> But we have this precious treasure [the good news about salvation] in [unworthy] earthen vessels [of human frailty], so the **grandeur and surpassing greatness of the power** will be [shown to be] **from God** [His sufficiency] **and not from ourselves**. (2 Cor. 4:7 AMP)

We don't have to hate where we feel weak. We don't have to defend it and tell others why we are actually right. Weakness is an outlet for God's greatness.

We just bring our weakness to the power source: Jesus. He helps us do what we need to from there, be it repent of sin, lean on Him, share with others, or do what seems impossible. He makes it easier. In my case, I eventually told my friend I'd twisted her words to mean something they didn't. I apologized, and I expected Jesus to redeem my unredeemable mistake. This friend and I are now closer than ever. She trusted me more after I was open and honest. She spoke life into my areas that needed real truth. I am stronger now because of it. God used her as a power source in my place of weakness.

What weakness have you been hiding? Keeping under wraps? Not sharing?

Do you feel like a bad parent? A lousy coworker? A bad communicator? An angry person? Selfish? Burdened by others? Bad in front of God?

What makes you feel weak? Maybe you hate how you feel?

May we, just for a moment, wipe one thing off our chalkboard of self-contention? Jesus doesn't hate emotions; He had them too.

> When [Jesus] saw the crowds, He was **moved with compassion for them**, because they were harassed and helpless, like sheep without a shepherd. (Matt. 9:36 BSB)
>
> Jesus saw the huge crowd as he stepped from the boat, and **he had compassion on them** and healed their sick. (Matt. 14:14)
>
> Jesus **wept**. (John 11:35)
>
> Jesus was **filled with the joy** of the Holy Spirit. (Luke 10:21)
>
> When Jesus saw her weeping and saw the other people wailing with her . . . he was **deeply troubled**. (John 11:33)
>
> As [Jesus] came closer to Jerusalem and saw the city ahead, he **began to weep**. (Luke 19:41–42)
>
> Jesus called his disciples and told them, "**I feel sorry** for these people. They have been here with me for three days, and they have nothing left to eat." (Matt. 15:32)
>
> Looking at the man, Jesus **felt genuine love** for him. (Mark 10:21)

[Jesus] told them, "**My soul is crushed with grief** to the point of death." (Matt. 26:38)

Some of us view emotions as burdens, or even sin. But Jesus was without sin—and Jesus got emotional. *We aren't bad or weak because we feel.* We need to stop hating our make-up when God made us this way. We are wise to stop demanding we feel a certain way. This is a breeding ground for anxiety and restlessness.

Jesus felt. He felt for the harassed. He had mercy for the helpless and compassion toward those in need. His feelings for others, at times, moved Him. He went through rejection, pain, sorrow, and abandonment.

Even God the Father is described as having feelings; He tells His chosen people, "You shall not worship any other god; for the LORD, whose name is Jealous, is a jealous (impassioned) God [demanding what is rightfully and uniquely His]" (Exod. 34:14 AMP). The Spirit is grieved (suffering tremendous I-miss-you sorrow) when we block Him out (Eph. 4:30). The Spirit even groans for us, interceding on our behalf. This has the sounds of feeling behind it.

What feelings are you stuffing down and away from yourself and God? Stop putting yourself through a beating because you have feelings. I believe God not only wants you to bring your "best" self to Him but also your *worst* self too. He can handle it. He can handle *you.* He is your Daddy, remember? Maybe He wants to give you a hug of sorts.

Good dads hold crying babies. They teach small children. They don't berate a child for missing the nail with the plastic hammer. They don't say, "Pull yourself together, get that food in your mouth, and stop being a whiner." Instead, drawing near, they take the fork of food the kid can't get to their mouth and help guide it in. Working together, the dad shows the kid how to do it.

Jesus says something similar to us: "Walk with me and work with me—watch how I do it" (Matt. 11:29 MSG).

I believe Jesus wants to walk with you through your weakness, not just snap you out of it. In love, He might want to teach you some things.

Healing

My husband and I have a one-minute, bring-it-to-light approach for weakness.

It works like this: suppose the enemy says to me, *Kelly, you are a bad mom. You blah, blah, blah . . .*

After asking God for forgiveness for anything I may have done wrong, if the enemy keeps harassing me this way, I say, "You know what? I agree with you. You are right. I am a bad mom. No one is good, not one. But, you know what? *Jesus!*"

Jesus! Jesus! Jesus!

Jesus *always* more than covers me; His grace is more than enough. His righteousness has become my righteousness. His words about me are true. His lovingkindness will lead me. His forgiveness is there for me—and so, Jesus! Jesus! Jesus!

Even if I feel powerless, Christ's love and blood powerfully overrule my worst thoughts about myself. His "surpassing greatness" of power (Ps. 150:2 NIV) subdues any lying voices.

The enemy has no claim left against me after I plead *Jesus.* After I say, "Jesus! Jesus! Jesus!" Jesus is the only case I have to stand on. I am not guilty because He is my evidence and my closing statement. I can trust God's verdict always stands: *Not guilty! Because of Jesus!*

In this, Jesus is always victorious. I am under Daddy's unconditional love. The assault is over. Here I can almost always find my way to new levels of recovery from sin and mistakes.

God said to Paul, who called himself a "chief sinner,"

My grace is sufficient for you [My lovingkindness and My mercy are more than enough—always available—regardless of the situation]; for [**My**] **power is being perfected [and is completed and shows itself most effectively] in [your] weakness.** (2 Cor. 12:9 AMP)

Our weakness becomes God's power showing itself. It is in this place that we begin to hear the heart of God remind us:

Even though you are weak, I have equipping power for you to take.

Even though you may still hate how you act, My mercy is for you.

Even though you think weakness makes you worthless, I can still work.

This abolishes self-pride, which says, "It's all up to me."

For it is by grace you have been saved, through faith—and this is not from yourselves—it is the gift of God, not by works, so that no one can boast. (Eph. 2:8–9 NIV)

God's perfecting has nothing to do with my power. His saving is a free gift I can't pay enough for.

His gift is so free, it's like I got a car, a house, a vacation, and every single thing I could ever want in my whole life gifted to me, even though I am the worst person in the world. That's what it's like. And I somehow also narrowly escape into heaven—forever. It is inconceivable. I'm entirely unworthy, and I get His best gifts.

I am weak, but Christ is strong to save. I am weak, but in Him I become strong.

This is why, after God talked to Paul about His sufficient grace, Paul resolved to "all the more gladly boast in my weaknesses, so that the power of Christ [may completely enfold me and] may dwell in me" (2 Cor. 12:9 AMP).

Somehow I think Paul knew boasting doesn't lead people to Jesus. Honesty about weakness does—for it shows the power of the gospel that saves, redeems, and restores. What greater testimony is there than what Christ has done for us?

It is through weakness that people see the power of Christ in such a way that they have to know, "How?" How did God do this? How did we get so transformed?

Weakness testifies of Jesus. Remember, at the end of us is more of God's rule (Matt 5:3 MSG). More of God's kingdom. God's kingdom is righteousness, peace, and joy (Rom. 14:17). These elements are the trifecta of rest.

Jesus said, "God blesses those who are poor and realize their need for him, *for the Kingdom of Heaven is theirs*" (Matt. 5:3).

It's okay to be weak and to need God. God blesses people like that.

To obtain greater rest, change how you think and speak *rest.* Make a decision to agree with what Jesus has done for you.

> When you feel weak and wounded, proclaim, "Let the weak say 'I am strong!'" (Joel 3:10 AMP).
>
> When you are at the end of yourself, tell your soul, "I may be at the end of myself, but I am at the start of God."
>
> When you feel as helpless as a child, remind yourself, "The Kingdom of God belongs to those who are like these children" (Luke 18:16).
>
> When you feel unsettled, tell yourself, "For the kingdom of God is . . . righteousness, peace and joy in the Holy Spirit" (Rom. 14:17 NIV).

David's psalms are famous for this sort of verbal professing and processing. So often, he would feel the unease of a turbulent situation. He would say, "I feel destroyed, ruined, or about to be crushed." But then he'd acknowledge God, saying something like, "The LORD is the stronghold of my life—of whom shall I be afraid?" (Ps. 27:1 NIV). Or he'd proclaim something like, "For in the day of trouble he will keep me safe in his dwelling; he will hide me in the shelter of his sacred tent and set me high upon a rock" (v. 5 NIV).

Then he'd praise God. David knew how to make soul-filling declarations to address soul-plundering situations. And he'd find rest again. No wonder David accomplished so much in his life—defeating giants, becoming king, and living as a man after God's own heart (1 Sam. 13:14).

Profess the Word of God from your mouth to help possess it in your heart.

prayer

Daddy, I need You. I don't feel like much. I feel small. I feel insignificant. I feel unworthy. I feel alone sometimes. I feel unsure. I don't always really know what I am doing. I want to be valuable. I want to do things that bless You, but somehow I am either not sure how or I just don't. What do You think of all this, of me?

And, despite all this, will You still use me? Love me? Am I still valuable to You? Will You reveal Your heart to me? Will You heal me when unbelief cripples me and keeps me from honesty? I know You are for me. I know You will help me. I put all my trust in You. Once again. In Jesus's name. Amen.

How to Stop Worrying and Think New Thoughts

When I feel weak, I worry. How about you? I think of ways that people might be judging me. I panic. I wonder if God will ever use me.

But feeling weak is a great opportunity to remember how Christ is strong. This helps me get back up again.

I remember:

I am full of Christ.
I am victorious through Christ.
I overcome because of Christ.

Jesus accepts me; He did not reject me on the cross.
Jesus leads me in my life.
Jesus made me into a new creation.

I am free of the past; the past is the past.
I am in the light, and the light gives me clarity on which direction to take.
I am controlled by the Spirit of power and love, not enslaved to a spirit of fear or timidity.

I am being perfected, as Christ is perfecting me.
I am learning and growing more loving because of Jesus.
I am becoming wiser with my words.

I am taking a stand against the enemy-accuser.
I have authority against powers of darkness, thanks to Jesus.
I am undone from shame, because Christ shamed the powers of darkness and death on the cross.

I can pray for deep relationships and cultivate them.
I am not alone, because God is with me.
I continually put my trust in God and stand in full hope of what's to come.

SIX

the way of humility

SIT IN GOD'S CARE

Serve God. Love others.

At church, I do everything I can to live this. As I approach the building, I'm already thinking about the folks I see by the door. *How can I uplift them? What do they need? How can God use me to change their day?* I am ready and prepared to give them what they need.

Even as I sit down, I look around the sanctuary to see who may need help, prayer, or wisdom. *Who needs anything?* Sometimes I get distracted from listening to the pastor. I can't stop thinking about others. What I should give to them. How I can better love them. If I should provide for them in some way. I get caught up in loving.

Not only that, I get caught up in working. I've always felt driven to be a super-hard worker. While some people got straight As without much effort, I'd study all night long to get As and Bs with an occasional C. I've had to work three times harder than average people. I know the value of effort.

Even when it comes to writing, I've had to work hard. Frankly, as a kid I wrote my letters backward, and I was tested to see if I had learning disabilities. I stayed back in third grade. One boss nearly tore up my work, she thought my writing was so bad. I know that what I do today is solely a gift from Jesus—but one I have to work at.

I steward things of God through hard work. This is what I've always done.

Except this season. This season, it is as if God has said to me, *Kelly, sit down and take a time-out.*

Our family recently moved, and no one knows me at my new church, so it's not so easy to help. No one is much aware of me, because it is a megachurch, so I just kind of sit there, not handing out much love. Not serving all the time. Not hearing, "Wow, Kelly, thank you so much for helping me!"

Even more, in my ministry work, things have gone silent. Speaking events have come in, but not that many. There is more sitting with God than there is running out and doing videos, sharing stuff on social media, and being "out there." I am in the quiet place, the hidden place.

In this place, I've gotten to thinking . . .

Am I still good even when I'm not doing good things? When people don't need me, when they don't say, "Oh, Kelly, I *really* needed that," when I don't feel the high of giving, when I don't provide others value, am I still good? Do I have value?

Am I finding my worthiness in works, or in Christ? It is easy to do so much good for Jesus that you start believing in your own goodness. I am finding this to be a big warning bell in my life. What matters is not what I do for Him but truly, deeply, and wholeheartedly knowing what He has done for me.

Am I important if I am unneeded and unknown? If no one but Jesus knows me, am I still known? Am I still valuable? Am I still important?

These sorts of questions make me ask other questions. *Is Jesus enough? Completely? Entirely? Solely? Without me even doing anything?*

Putting On a Show

I think, in some ways, I've put on a show of loving Jesus. It has been scary to recognize how I can act somewhat like the Pharisees in the New Testament.

> Everything they do is for show. On their arms they wear **extra wide prayer boxes** with Scripture verses inside, and they wear robes with **extra long tassels**. And they love to sit at the head table at banquets and in the seats of honor in the synagogues. They love to receive respectful greetings as they walk in the marketplaces, and to be called "Rabbi." (Matt. 23:5–7)

Through religious acts I can gain self-value. Just like the Pharisees. On face value, these people looked like they were doing everything right. They knew the Old Testament inside and out. They abided by it, as far as they could see. They did stuff for God. They were relevant to the religious culture of the day.

Yet somewhere along the line, their motives got mixed. Their tassels grew longer and longer and their prayer boxes got bigger and bigger. They carried Scripture—and completely missed the heart of the matter.

When your identity is based on what you do, you always have to keep on doing. When your worth is based on how you look, you always have to keep looking right. If you are good at loving, healing, or giving, it can be easy to walk just a little bit higher, a little taller, than everyone else.

Christian, beware.

Do you feel more spiritual than others? Are you always the giver and never the receiver? A good-doer and never a sitter? Continually needed but never in need?

To exalt yourself above the low ground at the foot of the cross is very risky business.

The Pharisees super-sized their spiritual appearance. They knew what was right. They had answers. So they judged, critiqued, and were offended by Jesus. His working on the Sabbath, His habit of eating with sinners, His healings and wonders—Jesus threatened their position.

Are you a Pharisee in some ways?

An easily offendable, critical, and know-it-all heart is a signal of a pharisaical heart, one that I have been guilty of carrying.

Do you have "exalted thoughts"?

I have all the answers.

I have it all together.

I am better off than they are.

I deserve better than this.

I want public recognition for what I do.

I want to be good so people think I am good.

I am worthy or valuable when I am adding value.

I want to be served, not serve.

Do you have "works-based thoughts"?

I must do ___ to get ___.

If you don't ___, you are a ___.

If I wear ___ or look like ___, then I am ___.

I do all this to the point of ___.

Do you have "prideful thoughts"?

I know what you need to do.

I know a lot more than others do.

I have the advice you need to make your world better.

I know that Bible story or lesson already.

If I see how bad you are, I feel better about myself.

If I have your answer, then I am smarter and spiritually better off than you.

I can't look weak or in need.

I care more about how you see me than about how God does.

Do you have "judgmental thoughts"?

I will set straight those who don't think (look, act, understand) exactly like me.

I will murder with my words those who haven't grasped what I've grasped.

I will punish those who appear to be threatening me.

Do you have "greedy thoughts"?

I need to be recognized or valued above everyone else.

I need a following to be known and recognized.

I want my appearance to show that I am better than you, so I feel better about myself.

Do you entertain "over-religious thoughts"?

My knowledge of Scripture should warrant prestige.

I research God's Word over giving heart devotion to it.

I speak things in the dark I wouldn't want anyone to hear me say in the light.

I must always set others straight.

Maybe you crave thank-yous, appreciation, a promotion, a better reputation, rewards, a better feeling about yourself, more admiration, good word of mouth, better earnings, being seen, a more influential life, or a destiny so great it stands out as a high tower. Maybe you want to appear strong, effective, or smart. Maybe you need to have all the answers, or you want to be independent in all your ways. Maybe you use God's Word in a know-it-all way.

You know, Jesus had strong feelings about the Pharisees. Listen to how Jesus talked about this group.

"You're hopeless! What arrogant stupidity!" (Matt. 23:16 MSG)

"Snakes!" (v. 33)

"Blind fools!" (v. 17)

"Sons of vipers!" (v. 33)

"Hypocrites!"(v. 27)

"Woe to you, teachers of the law and Pharisees." (v. 27)

"You are like whitewashed tombs, which look beautiful on the outside but on the inside are full of the bones of the dead and everything unclean." (v. 27 NIV)

He even stated the Pharisees made their converts into "twice as much a child of hell as [they] are" (v. 15 NIV).

This is scary. "God opposes the proud" (James 4:6).

I don't want God set against me. And I certainly don't want to be called any of those things. But when I make it more about "The Kelly Show" than I do about admitting the needs I have, being open, coming to terms with my weaknesses, and being humble, I can easily enter the red zone.

Then I start looking at people. They are doing *this* or *that*. They have tattoos and dance weird. They don't really know

God's Word right. They are grumpy, even though they go to church every week.

But I don't know their heart, nor what God is orchestrating in it.

Beware, ye hypocrite.

Anyone who claims to know all the answers doesn't really know very much. (1 Cor. 8:2)

Along this journey, I'm starting to realize, the more I know about God, the less I know. The more I think I can judge, the more I am in a horrible error of ways. The more I think I have everything figured out, the more I must admit I am only just beginning to learn.

I have judged someone in one category only to learn three weeks later they were right all along. Or I couldn't understand how anyone could ever do *this* or *that* but then I came to see all the reasons they did what they did. Or I decided that internet info was right about someone when I couldn't even see their heart. Whoops.

So, what I really know about God's Word is that I don't fully live God's Word. What I know about what I write in this book is that I don't have it all conquered. What I know about my judgment is that I sin just like the next girl.

And I need that next girl as much as she needs me. Because God uses the body of Christ, nearly as much as His Word and our prayers, to bring our breakthroughs. But there's no breakthrough if I never break down in need in front of others.

If I can't listen to and receive a sister's counsel too. I am not in this battle alone.

Receiving help is humility, and honesty matters. I don't have to prove myself. I am not required to overdo it and to overcompensate. I need no more than me and no less than Christ.

Paul said, "For I resolved to know nothing while I was with you except Jesus Christ and him crucified" (1 Cor. 2:2 NIV).

Like other people, I am in the sheep pen, as my friend Karen likes to say, with all the other sheep who desperately need Jesus too. We are all just following the Shepherd and trusting Him to watch over us and be the keeper of our souls (Ps. 121:5–6). If I were to try to keep myself, I'd be dead from an eating disorder by now.

I am just trying to love God and love others well, from an authentic heart. To be no more and no less than the truest me, whom Jesus loves abundantly.

Freedom

I am unconditionally loved, based on no work of my own (Eph. 2:8). This means nothing can earn me a better position.

It makes no sense to go to the judge like a convict on death row when he's already exonerated you. If you insist on working the food line in prison to earn good marks for an early release, that would be stupidity . . . if you already have freedom.

I have it all, in full.

There was a punishment; Jesus paid it.

There was a prison; Jesus shamed the powers of darkness to set me free from it.

There was a verdict; Jesus overruled it.

There was a consequence called hell; Jesus broke every prison bar to release me from it.

Now I walk as a new creation, dead to sin and alive to Christ. Filled by the Spirit. There is no hard work or hard time left. I depend on Christ's mighty power.

> That's why I work and struggle so hard, **depending on Christ's mighty power** that works within me. (Col. 1:29)

Everything else is striving, vanity, and selfish ambition.

Say you had a son who woke up every morning, took out the trash, unloaded the dishwasher, emptied the closets, and by afternoon had your cars washed. After all that, he came to you and said, "What else can I do to please you? I have to do more." How would you respond?

Likely you might say, "Sit down and rest a little while. You don't have to prove yourself all the time to me."

Your son is already loved. He has nothing left to prove to you. And, thanks to Christ, you have nothing left to prove to God.

Jesus loves you anyway.

How Do We Go from Here?

Humility does not have to be seen. It doesn't have to feel important. It doesn't have to be recognized. Or liked.

Whereas the Pharisees wanted to be seen and valued, true service to God doesn't need acclaim or fame. It knows God sees. It knows God rewards. It knows there is more to this world than the here and now. It doesn't rely on instant gratification.

1. Humility gives thanks for moments "unrecognized."

     Be it a prayer you prayed, a gift you gave, a word of life you offered—what is unseen by other people is seen by God.

> For there is nothing hidden that will not be disclosed, and nothing concealed that will not be known or brought out into the open. (Luke 8:17 NIV)

   When you do something for God, and with God, you can be 100 percent certain: you succeeded and God rewards. Every investment in His kingdom reaps eternal dividends.

   Even more, in the here and now, keep in mind that God sees and knows. A cloud of witnesses watches you. God roots for you. He knows your heart. He wants your success in all His ways. He is on your side.

2. Humility rests under the highness of God.

   I love how Dr. David Jeremiah put it in his commentary on Galatians 6, as he spoke about how some of us may not be in the spotlight or may not feel needed, but—here's what I love—"when we join in the ministry of others with our hearts and our hands, our [unseen, personal, or small] ministry is just as

important as theirs [big, powerful, growing, or small],
and He blesses it in the same way."[1]

Whether our act touches one or five thousand.
Whether other people notice or not. Whether it gains
us friends or actually pushes us into a neighbor-
hood where we work all alone. When we stick with
what God is doing and what He is calling us to do,
independent of the size, we get a good thing.

> Day and night I'll stick with GOD;
>> I've got a good thing going and I'm not letting
>> go. (Ps. 16:8 MSG)

> Take delight in the LORD,
>> and he will give you your heart's desires.
>> (Ps. 37:4)

3. To have humility is to be no more or no less than who
   I am today.

   I can't be more loved than I already am. I can't be
   more beautiful than I am in Christ. I can't be more
   whole than wholly loved. I try to dwell on these
   things as I make decisions, talk to people, and consider what to do. I let them belong to my soul and
   direct my day.

> God is there, ready to help;
> I'm fearless no matter what.
> Who or what can get to me? (Heb. 13:6 MSG)

God is my direction, not other people. Righteousness, peace, and joy lead me, not pressures from others. I am happy.

> I'm happy from the inside out,
>   and from the outside in, I'm firmly formed.
> [Jesus] canceled my ticket to hell—
>   that's not my destination!
> Now [God's] got my feet on the life path,
>   all radiant from the shining of [God's] face.
> Ever since [He] took my hand,
>   I'm on the right way. (Ps. 16:9–12 MSG)

Rest is knowing that all I need, I have in Christ. Rest is internal and eternal security. It beholds the Master, and it carries on.

prayer

God, I confess the many ways I have made my works, my knowledge, and my insight far more about me than about You. I am so sorry. I am not an island of wisdom or a treasure trove of all Your ways. I am a daughter who needs connection with You and others. I have distanced myself from You. I have created walls between me and others. I haven't wanted to be hurt. Forgive me for acting as I have. Forgive me for setting myself up against You. I don't want to do this anymore. Right now, I humble myself before You. You are mighty to change me. You are the answer I need. Show me every way within me that needs to come into more alignment with You. I do not profess to know it all, for You know everything. I ask You to pour out grace on me so that my heart may continually stay softened and pliable in Your hands. I want to be moldable so that I can be shaped into Your image, not hard and cracked any longer. Thank You for loving me no matter what. Thank You for putting people around me who have the answers to my questions. Thank You for teaching me. It is an honor to be Your servant, Your faithful daughter, and Your beloved. Teach me, Teacher. In Jesus's name. Amen.

Humility Is . . .

- Taking the low seat.
- Listening and learning.
- Waiting.
- Saying less to love more.
- Helping.
- Being authentic and vulnerable.
- Obeying to the point of awkwardness.
- Seeking God on your face or knees.
- Allowing God to reach to the seediest and sleaziest places of your soul.
- Resting on the foundations of Jesus: you are loved, saved, and wanted because of His blood.
- Having faith, no matter what you see.

- Trusting Jesus is the only way.
- Leaning on God more than yourself.
- Knowing Jesus alone is worthy of praise.
- Serving in the unseen.
- Trashing your natural mind for the Spirit mind.
- Needing Jesus's breakthrough.
- Constantly refocusing on Jesus.
- Resting without needing "to do."
- Trusting God to save you, today and for eternity.
- Believing you are who God says you are.
- Taking life one day at a time (without running ahead).
- Laying down timelines to trust God's time.
- Realizing you don't need to understand.
- Asking for help or withholding help.
- Practicing forgiveness right now.
- Deciding *not* to partner with offense.
- Promoting others.
- Realizing your way may not be the best way.
- Being okay with not having the answer.
- Understanding the story is not all about you.

SEVEN

the way of forgiveness

EMBRACE GOD'S COMPASSION

In the past, I've done informal counseling sessions with people. Usually we just plop ourselves down on a church couch and I listen. I pray. With God, people come to see things they may not have before.

Anyway, after dozens of such hours spent sitting with people, I've come to see one common issue. No matter what background, culture, or economic strata the person came from, if they have unrest, they almost always have unforgiveness. And since rest is what we're after, the unrest of unforgiveness must be undone.

Many say to me, "Oh, Kelly, I've forgiven already. I'm good there." Then they'll go on and tell me about how they feel angry at others, rejected by how people have acted, and frustrated at God.

These are things that make me go, "Hmm."

Maybe we say we've forgiven, but have we *really* forgiven? Are you struggling with:

- Bitterness that life hasn't gone as you wanted?
- Resentment toward yourself or others?
- Anger at what you've done or how someone "took advantage" of you?
- Thoughts of retaliation?
- Fantasies where others find out how good you are or how bad they were?
- Fear that you may repeat the sin you committed before?
- The hope that you will someday come back and "prove them all wrong"?
- Overwhelming feelings of abandonment, rejection, or self-frustration?

Unforgiveness can be tied to illness, such as stress linked to heart disease, asthma, obesity, diabetes, headaches, depression, gastrointestinal problems, Alzheimer's disease, accelerated aging, and premature death.[1]

And bitterness causes something almost as bad.

We've all seen a bitter person. The deep lines indented around their face where their smile used to be. The way they can't seem to muster up a glimmer in their eye. The way they moan. The way they don't want to face people anymore. The sourness on their tongue. Many times they don't even realize how bad they've gotten.

God warns us of bitterness—the sour building up of resentment, irritation, and annoyance targeted toward another person. "See to it that no one falls short of the grace of God and that *no bitter root* grows up to cause trouble and defile many" (Heb. 12:15 NIV).

To *defile*, according to Merriam-Webster, means "to make unclean or impure . . . to violate the sanctity of: desecrate."[2] I don't want to be desecrated in God's eyes, do you?

What a tragedy it is to choose to desecrate yourself with the *ick* of unforgiveness.

My Forgiveness Problem

To forgive, I often think of who has offended me. I say, "I forgive (so and so)." I tell God, "I let them go." I want their burden off my shoulders. I remove the offense.

But sometimes my mind wanders back. Sometimes I get stuck on Facebook looking at their page. Sometimes I compare how they are doing with how I am doing. Sometimes I think of how much I would appreciate them telling me they were sorry.

When this happened recently, I inquired of God, "Father, how do I know when I've really forgiven?"

I discerned His reply within my heart: *Kelly, when you can love them again.*

This stopped me in my tracks. *Am I loving these people again? Truly? Deeply? Wholeheartedly? Even from a distance?*

I took a second to be honest with myself.

Am I wanting their increase, even above my own? *Not really. I want to show them I don't need them and that I'm doing fine without them.*

Am I praying for them—even to the point of them doing better than me? *No. I hope, because of God's justice, He'll lift me up and hold them back.*

Am I wanting sympathy from others due to this offense? *Sometimes it feels really good to tell others what happened so I can be reminded of how right I am.*

Am I able to stop talking and ruminating about old grievances, so I can understand God's heart? *Not always. Sometimes I can't stop thinking about how I got hurt, over and over again.*

Am I okay with them never, ever, realizing they were wrong? *No. It feels like no one is taking care of me. They get away with it and I am left on the hook with these icky feelings.*

Am I able to only speak good things to others about them? *No. I don't want anyone else to be hurt or impacted; I want everyone to know what this person has done.*

Love "keeps no record of wrongs" (1 Cor. 13:5 NIV). Love "does not demand its own way" (v. 5). Love is not "resentful" (v. 5 ESV). "Love is patient, love is kind" (v. 4 NIV). Love "is not puffed up" (v. 4 BSB).

"Love covers all transgressions" (Prov. 10:12 BSB).

The Hard Truth

God is patient. Jesus doesn't post my sin on the nightly news. Nor does He announce it on Facebook. He doesn't staple my past to my forehead.

Never once has God come into my life when I was making a mistake, got all up in my face, and demanded that I apologize. He is "compassionate and gracious, slow to anger, abounding in love" (Ps. 103:8 NIV) toward me—and toward my offender. At the same time, He is righteous and just.

I want to be like Jesus.

> Don't you see how wonderfully kind, tolerant, and patient God is with you? Does this mean nothing to you? Can't you see that **his kindness is intended to turn you from your sin**? (Rom. 2:4)

Think about your life. Has God been patient with you? Does He give you room to discover and uncover His ways? Has someone ever borne up under you during a time when you felt like you were just inching along? How did that feel? Has anyone ever given you something good you felt you didn't deserve? How did it impact you? How far have you come, due to the kindness of Jesus on the cross? Take a second to count the ways. This exercise matters.

We can truly, deeply, and wholeheartedly forgive, because we've been truly, deeply, and wholeheartedly forgiven by Christ. There's no greater love than this.

> There is no greater love than to lay down one's life for one's friends. (John 15:13)

117

Forgiveness is a release of heaviness.

Because Jesus laid down His life for us, we lay down our grievances. We don't carry them anymore.

Now, I know this can be hard when someone has abused you, used you, or broken you catastrophically. I get it. I really do. But let me clarify: loving has different distances when coupled with wisdom. God may desire you to limit your proximity, schedule, or face time with someone. Yet this doesn't mean you can't still love them. The main point of resurrecting "love," through the act of forgiveness, is so you can once again desire God's very best for a person. And mean it. With absolute trueness of heart.

Do not make excuses for why you can't forgive. The person forgiveness most frees is *you.*

The Application of Forgiveness

Let's walk through forgiveness so you can finally get the weight of everyone else's problems off your chest. Doing this will provide you with new air to breathe and soul recovery that brings peace and rest to your life.

In order to help you identify who you need to forgive and for what, consider a few more questions:

- Is there a person you tend to critique? Or someone you avoid seeing?
- Do you get icky or frustrated feelings when you cross paths with a specific person?

118

- Do you think of one event over and over again?
- Do you repeatedly tell people about how someone hurt you?
- Do you continually feel guilty?
- Do you act passive-aggressively, overreact, or become triggered easily?
- Do you tend to undervalue another person's opinion because of what they've "done"?
- Do you fantasize about another's demise, or them getting "caught"?
- Do you want a person to see you as better than you are?
- Do you have a hard time blessing anyone?

If you answered *yes* to any of these, consider who your *yes* relates to. Likely there is some forgiveness work that needs to be done there.

That person might be completely and totally wrong, and yet you still need to forgive, even if they:

Never got caught.

Never said sorry.

May still hurt others.

Appear to have gotten away with it.

Don't even realize what they did.

Are arrogant or prideful.

Are still doing what you hate.

119

Yes, you may have some forgiveness work to do with that very person.

At this point, some icky feelings may be surfacing in you. *How could they? I wasn't doing anything wrong. I can't believe* ____. *It shouldn't be this way.*

First, I want to acknowledge your hurt. In this emotional place, I wish I could stop and give you a big hug. I know it hurts. It stinks. It's rotten that it happened. It's annoying that we all don't love each other better. I understand your feelings. It really is okay to cry. I want you to know that. Beyond this, the flesh side of me wants to fix everything for you, to rush in with some Clorox and a red bow to tie it up. Frankly, there is some trauma so deep that counseling really can help. And I know this from personal experience. It has helped me get on my way toward forgiveness.

Letting go is soul rest. It is recovering joy. It is rediscovering old relationships—or deciding not to. Either way, whether you reconnect with the person or not, forgiveness releases the baggage of yesterday to help you walk into a better today.

If you still feel stuck because you still feel angry, here is a tip: forgive without conditions.

Unconditional forgiveness sounds a lot like Jesus: "Father, forgive them, for they don't know what they are doing" (Luke 23:34).

Notice Jesus didn't say, "Forgive them after they realize they're acting like barbarians," or "Forgive them after they attend church, stop messing up, and start getting their act

together." Jesus basically said, "These people don't even realize the horrible thing they're doing, but Father, will You, in
all Your mercy, please remove all account of their mess-ups
entirely?"

Because of Jesus's unconditional saving, we are saved.
Because of His unconditional love, we can unconditionally
forgive. Unconditional forgiveness has no conditions tied
to it.

Many people have no idea how much they've actually hurt
us. We are all blind to others, to a degree. You probably
haven't set out to hurt someone—but you have.

We can be like Jesus, though, and choose to enter into rest
again through forgiveness.

Jesus didn't wait for long apologies. He didn't grandstand
or demand that we explain our every motive and mistake. He
didn't call for new theology and law, right then and there.
He didn't turn away from the very cross that, indeed, felt like
the death of Him.

He went straight into it—through the pain, the ridicule, and
the heartbreak—and chose to forgive anyway. For some of us,
forgiveness may feel like the death of us too. That's okay. Die
to your flesh. I assure you: it will bring life to you.

Jesus resurrects.

So, requiring nothing of them, needing no apology—moving
beyond your fantasies of justice, aside from your fear it may
happen again, apart from your uncertainty of where it goes
from here, beyond the anger that has fed your pain for so
long—and choosing to be more than the thoughts that keep
you stuck in the past, *forgive.*

It will be one of the best things you have ever done for yourself.

But love [that is, unselfishly seek the best or higher good for] your enemies, and do good, and lend, expecting nothing in return; for your reward will be great (rich, abundant), and you will be sons of the Most High; because He Himself is kind and gracious and good to the ungrateful and the wicked. Be merciful (responsive, compassionate, tender) just as your [heavenly] Father is merciful. (Luke 6:35–36 AMP)

When You Need God's Forgiveness

If I've seen it once, I've seen it a thousand times. A person asks God to forgive them but never actually receives God's forgiveness by allowing themselves to *feel forgiven*. So they become weighed down. They choose shame. They keep repeating the same errors. They get blocked from greater opportunities. They miss deep connection with God. They fall prey to the enemy's voice. They are deterred from sharing Jesus with others. And they hate themselves for all this. They become self-critical and feel they are a "bad Christian."

This is a tragedy. Believing in the bad, they hold themselves back from the new. New hope. New relationship dynamics. New growth.

Yet it doesn't have to be this way. "It is for freedom that Christ has set us free. Stand firm, then, and do not let yourselves be burdened again by a yoke of slavery" (Gal. 5:1 NIV).

Jesus *has set* you free. This work is done. This act is completed. Don't go back to an old yoke of shame when He has already forgiven you. He said, "It is finished" (John 19:30). And it is. His forgiveness is permanent, unconditional, and everlasting for those who ask for and receive it.

Old yokes enslave people to lesser lives. Christ died to give you far more.

Jesus completely forgives us. Jesus completely purifies us. Jesus "has removed our sins as far as the east is from the west" (Ps. 103:12). If God keeps no remembrance of your wrongs, why should you? Let it come off you.

Forgive yourself, like Christ already has.

> Heal me, LORD, **and I will be healed**;
>   save me and I will be saved,
>   for you are the one I praise. (Jer. 17:14 NIV)

Going Deeper Still

Forgiving others and yourself is good, but it often is not good enough. There is one more step.

I figured this out only recently, as I was sitting on my bed. "There's still something more, something missing," I said to my husband. "It's as if years of rejection and abandonment have made me feel like I am always about to be abandoned. I have forgiven the people, but I am still expecting the problem to repeat itself. I can almost feel bad things coming toward me."

Not long after this conversation, I read the highly recommended book *Total Forgiveness* by R. T. Kendall, which gave me much insight. As I pondered my own fear that my history would repeat itself, I was struck by his words: "[God] sometimes appears to us to have been unfair, [but] we must relinquish our bitterness and wholly forgive Him before we can move on with our lives."[3]

What? Forgive God? I hadn't even considered this.

I would never, ever, have admitted I was angry at God. But I suppose I was.

Underneath a thousand levels of denial, I was angry. Although I can now see the error of my ways, I couldn't explain why a good God would permit so much bad stuff to happen to me. While I knew there was sin, the world, and the devil to account for much strife, at the same time I couldn't banish the fact that God still permitted it. This was my gripe.

If it happened before, what will stop Him from allowing it to happen again? This was my deepest fear. It is what made my mind circle the same camp of defeat, discouragement, and demotivation—more times than I'd like to admit.

Are you afraid that history will repeat? That you will always be hurt?

Perhaps start with forgiving God for what appears to be neglect (although it 100 percent is *not*) or repeated pain. Then acknowledge His good ways: what you saw as neglect may actually be His heart to protect.

For example, God protects us by:

1. Keeping us alive. You are still breathing, aren't you? Imagine all the ways He kept things from getting far worse.

2. Doing what is best for us. We may hate the fact that we keep getting a shot in the arm, year after year, while God may be thinking, *I'm protecting her from getting the flu.* God knows why He does what He does.

3. Preparing us to authentically love others. If I tried to write this book without living through the turmoil and the trials of unconditional love, for instance, my words would fall flat.

Today I can say that reconciliation with God and others has fostered a sort of spiritual acceleration, both in my life and with others. Truly, "In all things God works for the good of those who love him, who have been called according to his purpose" (Rom. 8:28 NIV).

Not an ounce of anything is wasted in God's economy. All of it will come full circle to fulfill His every good purpose. And good is *good* with God. I don't know about you, but this gives me assurance.

My faith is more than my history; it is God's story in action. Just as Job said, "The LORD gave and the LORD has taken away" (Job 1:21 NIV), and just as Shadrach, Meshach, and Abednego replied to King Nebuchadnezzar, "But even if [God] doesn't [save us from this blazing furnace], we want you to know, Your Majesty, that we will not serve your gods or worship the image of gold you have set up" (Dan. 3:18 NIV), I can say, "God, even though I've been through it, no matter what, I still trust and love You."

I can forgive, even when I don't even know why I am doing it. Jesus is that good.

And without faith it is impossible to please God, because anyone who comes to him must believe that he exists and that **he rewards those who earnestly seek him**. (Heb. 11:6 NIV)

Despite *them* and what happened, God only has the best for me. I know He cares. I know it will all work out.

To let go of the past is to really begin to seize your future.

Forgiveness Maintenance

About two weeks ago, I was seated next to a man on an airplane who explained to me how his wife had cheated on him. He told me, "I could never, ever forgive her."

He went on to tell me how he could not find the "right" woman. This wasn't a surprise. Unforgiveness doesn't let you move on.

So I asked him if, right then on that airplane, he might forgive his wife? He said, "I can't. It's not the time. Plus, I don't even think of her and what she did."

The irony was, his wife's cheating was the first thing he rushed to talk to me about on that airplane. It didn't matter; he had convinced himself unforgiveness was serving him well.

I knew it wasn't. It was holding him back from love, keeping him angry, and making him rattle off irritations to strangers. What really stood out to me about this man was that he hadn't walked in unforgiveness for days but *years*. He let a root of bitterness grow. What a pity. What I discerned in minutes was years of torment for him.

Don't allow offense or bitterness to pile up. Refuse that, and reject the unrest that comes with it. Instead, with an inner determination, permit the enemy no ground. See people as Christ sees them: redeemable. See yourself as Christ sees you: forgivable.

Live a forgiveness lifestyle. Be unoffendable. Give out as much grace as you want to receive. This will keep you near the Prince of Peace—and His peace will keep flowing through you.

prayer

Father God, help me to love those who hurt me. This can be so hard.

The pain is real. I feel ___. I am upset that they ___. But Father, I forgive. I forgive because Christ forgave me. I forgive because this unforgiveness is only heaping unrest and confusion upon my own life. I give (insert their name) to you. I hand over all the ways they have ___. I ask You to give me a heart of grace toward them in coming days and wisdom to know how to handle them in order to protect my heart. I ask You to bless (insert their name). I ask You to increase their land and to love them. I ask You to help me so that I can finally move forward with You, into all You have for me.

In Jesus's name. Amen.

Rise above the Shame

Lunacy would be daily spanking your kid for an issue you forgave weeks ago. Can you imagine what message this would send to your kid? The guilt they'd still feel? They may start to believe, *I'll never stop doing wrong. Clearly, I can't*. They might think they can never change, even if they haven't taken cookies from the cookie jar recently.

Not forgiving yourself is the equivalent of this. It heaps shame on yourself that says, *You'll never get past this issue*. This is not of God. But you can rise above the shame.

1. **Be resolute** that asking for forgiveness means God (immediately) forgives it.

   He will not always accuse,
   nor will he harbor his anger forever;
   he does not treat us as our sins deserve
   or repay us according to our iniquities. . . .
   as far as the east is from the west,
   so far has he removed our transgressions from us. (Ps. 103:9–12 NIV)

2. **Go forth**, believing God above (or more than) your bad feelings.

3. **Rest** in God's ability to purify you.

   If we confess our sins, he is faithful and just and will forgive us our sins and purify us from all unrighteousness. (1 John 1:9 NIV)

4. **Embrace** God's best. Give thanks for His help. Rejoice over His cover. Walk in the freedom of His saving grace. Praise His ability to fully release you. See yourself as righteous right now, solely because of Jesus.

EIGHT

the way of focus

BECOME WORRY-FREE
AND PEACE-FILLED

I had a nagging, unsettled feeling.

Why? I couldn't place it. I was just on Facebook. Was it something there? I thought back to what I'd read:

A post slamming the brand of mac and cheese I buy. Apparently, it has cancer-causing toxins. My heart started pumping harder.

A post by a mom who found a copperhead snake in her garage attached to a glue mat. She warned, "If you don't want a snake in your child's bed, get this mat."

Fantastic. I need a snake mat now. I felt fear course up my arm.

An upset mom on a popular mom-page. The other moms at the bus stop were gossiping about her, saying, "Who wears short-shorts like that? And to a Christian school, after all?" The hurt mom wrote a post to defend her faith, saying, "Whatever! God loves me anyway." I pulled my shirt down over my slightly protruding belly.

All three posts stressed me out. *Now I have to worry that mac and cheese will poison my kids, snakes will attack them at night, and the moms at my kids' school will judge me for wrong outfit choices. Great.*

This isn't even to speak of the all-star women I just saw on my Facebook feed too: one on vacation in Africa, another at a party I wasn't invited to, and one changing the world. All the while, I'm standing there scrolling, somewhere between putting the laundry away and unloading the dishwasher. *Great.*

This social media stuff is mostly just a time-suck.

Extra three minutes? I scroll.

Bored? I scroll.

Tired? I scroll.

As if pockets of scrolling bring me rest and recovery . . . as if all this time, totaling hours each week, is adding to my life. My soul.

Social media is an ever-present distraction keeping me from peaceful heart-connection with God.

May I Vent for a Moment?

I have a love/hate relationship with social media. Some days I'd boycott it altogether. And some days I'd feel guilty about my absence and return to it, like a bad boyfriend.

I am aware of what it does.

> It pulls us in, because it's created to make us addicted to the feeling of scrolling.
>
> It exalts contention, raising up divisive and anger-inducing posts so they show up first.
>
> It knows what moves us emotionally, and through its algorithm, it apparently triggers us.
>
> It divides our insides, emotionally, as we see picture-perfect posts more than real-life ones.
>
> It is a time suck, wasting away our life, our moments, our dreams . . . as we watch someone else live "their best one."

Even programmer Kevin Holesh noted via his app, Moment, that "88% [of people scrolled] more than an hour a day, with the average being three hours. The typical user checked their phone 39 times in 24 hours. By comparison, in 2008, before smartphones became widespread, adults spent just 18 minutes a day on their phone."[1]

Grr. It is easy for me to blame social media. And I really, really want to go on doing so.

But it is me who willingly participates in all this. Who chooses to get caught up in thoughts like *Why does that one friend never like my posts?* or *How many comments do I have?* As if that somehow warrants the worth of my words. Or *How come Christians are raging against Christians like this?* And I let it bother me all afternoon.

It is also me who chooses to hide my inner loneliness by hopping online to fantasy land—where I see beautiful bodies, perfect outfits, gorgeous hair, and abundantly lovely holiday tables. As if people's picture-perfect moments make me feel less lonely and better about myself.

The issue comes down to my choices—what I choose to look at.

The eye is the lamp of your body. When your eye is clear [spiritually perceptive, focused on God], your whole body also is full of light [benefiting from God's precepts]. But when it is bad [spiritually blind], your body also is full of darkness [devoid of God's word]. Be careful, therefore, that the light that is in you is not darkness. So if your whole body is illuminated, with no dark part, it will be entirely bright [with light], as when the lamp gives you light with its bright rays. (Luke 11:34–36 AMP)

This makes me wonder—am I filling my moments with light or with darkness? With all-surpassing peace or with increasing worry? With God's light that makes me shine bright or with distraction that keeps me scrolling and busy?

Often what we think is rest is just busywork. Let's not choose complacency over connection with God.

132

Other Distractions

There's more to this distraction issue. It's not just social media that gets me distracted and out of focus, it is a whole bunch of other things. I sit down with my Bible, but before two minutes have passed my kids are asking me for breakfast. I walk into the kitchen to look out the window to reflect on God, but I see the messy counter, so I address it. I start to do some work, only to hear the "ding" of my phone, and I start texting. I think sending Christmas cards is a good idea, but I end up on Amazon for hours, trying to find the right pajamas. I plan to take a walk today with God, but I see a messy shelf, and I reorganize it.

It doesn't end in my house, either; distraction continues with other people. I am in the middle of a deep conversation and then talk about some random thing I need to do today. I begin to have a deep conversation with my kids but then I say, "By the way, you really need to clean this room."

Distraction around us can lead to distraction within us, if we are not careful. It can make us say:

I don't have enough time.

There is no space in my life.

I have so much to do.

People or needs are taking up the precious moments I
    desperately need.

Without even realizing it, we can transfer blessed time God has given us for rushed moments. Then we pay the price—with panic and worry.

Do you see the slippery slope of slight distractions and their impact? Are you distracted by:

- People who work their way into your life?
- People you *have to* keep up with?
- Phone calls, texts, or messages?
- Housework?
- Colleagues who need things—now?
- Social media?
- What other people are doing?
- What you should be doing?

This list could go on and on. Little distractions subtract big meaning from our life. It happens subtly. You give an inch and they take a mile.

But I learned something, about a year ago, that started to change my life in this department. It is called "deep work." The idea behind deep work is that it gives your mind room to think deeply. Rather than sitting down in a sea of distraction, you can clear the muddy waters so you can pursue what matters most.

Cal Newport, author of the book *Deep Work*, defines it as:

Activities performed in a state of distraction-free concentration that push your cognitive capabilities to their limit. These efforts create new value, improve your skill, and are hard to replicate. It's a skill that allows you to quickly master complicated information and produce better results in less time.

Deep work will make you better at what you do and provide the sense of true fulfillment that comes from craftsmanship. In short, deep work is like a super power.[2]

Some of you may be like me: you aren't working to conquer nuclear engineering in a world peace sort of way, but you want to conquer peace and focus in your life, with Christ. Deep work is for *us*. It is about silencing the shallow distractions of life to press into what is deep, meaningful, and blessed. It allows us to perform small tasks at peak levels of performance, taking less time and thus creating more space and peace in our life.

Deep work is intentionality. It helps us know what we are focusing on, so we *can* focus. It allows us to be present. If we are playing with our kids, we can be fully there, with God. If we are working, we can be deeply enmeshed in that. If we are listening to our parents, we can deeply listen.

For me, writing a book that is powerful to you, the reader, is of vital importance to me, so I choose to work deeply. This means turning my phone to silent. This means moving into a space away from my kids. This means not stopping to call a friend. This means not getting caught up in online stories that try to lure me in. This means trying not to flip over to my email account. This means keeping my mind focused on the work at hand. And when I do this, I can usually finish in two hours what would otherwise take ten! Thus after I'm done I have more time to meet with my family in the kitchen to make (toxic) mac and cheese.

Deep work knows when to shut work off too.

Do you see the power here? Ask yourself these three questions to begin to implement deep work in your life:

1. What is meaningful to me? (family, get-togethers with friends, focused time with your kids, Bible time with God)
2. What is distracting me from doing it? (errands, fear, text messages, phone calls, house chores, things you need to do)
3. How can I turn that distraction off—rework it, work around it, or work with it? (reschedule things, move things around, turn stuff off, tell people no, maintain a list, make new habits, establish a new routine, set aside intentional hours of focus, schedule a window of time to tackle the distraction)

To cultivate what is most important is to live a life of great importance. Then moments have meaning. We give ourselves permission to be where we *are*. When we're with our family, we can truly be with them. And when we're on a date with our spouse, we can be there too. And when we're with God, we'll really be with God.

Working Deeply with God

Deep work is great. But, at the same time, your best-laid plans can get busted. For example, right now I am homeschooling my kids due to the quarantine caused by the coronavirus pandemic, and they keep interrupting my deep writing work. There is grace for that. God knows my situation; He knows yours too. There is not always an optimal working environment. This is okay. Don't get jaded or irritated. Accept God's grace and peace and carry on.

If you feel worried about your lack of focus on what you are accomplishing or how you are connecting with God, let me assure you of one important thing: God has given us a "worry-free plan."

It starts with what we do.

Don't worry about anything; instead, **pray about everything**. Tell God what you need, and thank him for all he has done. (Phil. 4:6)

What we are to do is not worry. The second you fret, cast that feeling down. Don't agree with panic, stress, or pressures. You are under the grace of God, not the world's pressure. What is the worst-case scenario if something does not work out?

It moves to how we think.

Fix your thoughts on what is true, and honorable, and right, and pure, and lovely, and admirable. Think about things that are excellent and worthy of praise. (v. 8)

Choose to stay on this mind path. Encourage yourself along the way. Good thoughts produce good results.

137

It ends with what God does.

Then you will **experience God's peace**, which exceeds anything we can understand. His peace will guard your hearts and minds as you live in Christ Jesus. (v. 7)

Then the God of peace will be with you. (v. 9)

Spiritual deep work is our best work; it guards our heart and mind in Christ Jesus.

Invite the Holy Spirit to take your mind to a place of focus—to heavenly places and spaces, to pictures of grace and space, to holy lands of Bible promises and His Word in action.

Think about the things of heaven, not the things of earth. (Col. 3:2)

Worry pictures what's bad; let God's Word encourage you in what is good. It is okay to mentally escape into the heart and stories of God for just a little while.

Biblical hero David did just this. Sure, he conquered mighty giants and reigned as king. But, as evidenced in Psalm 23, he also knew how to envision God's green pastures and still waters. I imagine this was a way of escape for him—a place of solace in the midst of hard times.

Why not try to visualize yourself in this psalm? Why not get away a little? Why not remember this place when worries start to mount?

Let this psalm be the starting place of focus for you. Deep focus. Deep work. Deep rest. Deep connection with a God who leads you to restorative places. Come away with God . . .

Psalm 23

The Lord is my Shepherd [to feed, to guide and to
   shield me],
I shall not want.

He lets me lie down in green pastures;
He leads me beside the still and quiet waters.

He refreshes and restores my soul (life);
He leads me in the paths of righteousness
for His name's sake.

Even though I walk through the [sunless] valley of the
   shadow of death,
I fear no evil, for You are with me;
Your rod [to protect] and Your staff [to guide], they
   comfort and console me.

You prepare a table before me in the presence of my
   enemies.
You have anointed and refreshed my head with oil;
My cup overflows.

Surely goodness and mercy and unfailing love shall
   follow me all the days of my life,
And I shall dwell forever [throughout all my days]
   in the house and in the presence of the Lord.
   (AMP)

prayer

God, what do You have for me? Sometimes, I feel I can't hear You over everyone else's voice. It is hard to know what You have for me in the midst of a world moving a million miles an hour. Will You come and help me? Lead me? Show me? What should I be partaking in, and what should I let go? What should I make my focus in life, and what is a lesser thing? In Jesus's name. Amen.

Keeping Focus When People Demand Much of You

People often have unsaid expectations that need to be addressed. They may want you to do something—or come with requests they want you to address—*now!*

If you do everything for everyone, you will have no time. But if they don't know what to expect from you, they may keep asking you. If you leave your intentions vague, you may hit increasing problems and find distraction presses up right against your heels.

A good way to keep focus is to handle people's expectations in advance.

How to Handle People's Expectations

1. **Behold** them. Understand the small inkling inside of you that says someone may have an unsaid expectation of you. Acknowledge that you have expectations of your own, and that it is okay to express those too.

Note: You may first acknowledge this within yourself as nervousness or anxiousness. This is because you usually do not confront unsaid expectations that you or others have.

2. **Confirm** them. Have a sit-down meeting with the person. Ask them, "Do you want ___ from me? Is how I am seeing things correct?"

   Or tell them, "I need ___ from you. It will help me ___."

   Let them know what you can or cannot do. Let them know how you operate, and what you need from them in order to preserve focus and deep work. Give them timeframes they can reach out to you. Set the foundations.

3. **Check in** with the person. Plan to meet up again to see how things are going.

NINE

the way of less

ENJOY THE PRESENCE OF GLADNESS

The lie: have more, be happier.

I should know. I had "more," including a huge house, two luxury cars, two kids, and a private school for my kids, yet I wasn't happier. My husband wasn't happier because of "stuff," either.

The whole time we had this "more," groundhogs dug up the yard, making me constantly afraid I'd have to shell out big bucks to fix the landscaping. Bats invaded the attic; we had to get a guy in a hazmat suit to come over to scoop out the poop. A flood happened in the super large basement; I spent countless hours on the phone with the insurance company trying to settle a claim.

Just because we have "more" doesn't mean we get more joy. Ownership is not happiness. Just ask someone who owns debt.

At this time, we owned a whole bunch of furniture too. In that house on the hill, we hired a lady to help us get "the look" everyone else had. She showed us pictures of beautiful rugs, and we selected one that had gray woven fabric; it was expensive. Four years later, it wouldn't fit our new home, so it was left out near the curb, getting rained on. We drove off with thousands of dollars left behind us in the rearview mirror. Our other high-end furniture got dented from move after move. It was just stuff. But it also cost money I could have more wisely spent—or given to others—for sure.

In all this, and because we've moved to something like nine states in a little more than ten years, I've realized I don't need much to get by. Without stuff anchoring me, I am able to travel and to move where God wants me to go. Nothing holds me. This is freedom.

Somewhat by necessity, I now have less than a handful of sweaters. Less toys. Less stuff.

Also less folding. Less ties to *things*. Less to think about. Less to clean. Less to organize. And more ability to be present. More time for meaningful relationship. More space for God.

Our Obsession with Acquisition

Culture tells us we need an "acquire more" lifestyle. Buy more. Get more. Upsize our house. The only thing is, when we upsize our house, we also upsize our neighbors. Once we see what they have, there is a tendency to want it. To get a car like theirs.

To decorate our home like theirs. To have a watch like theirs. To landscape our yard like theirs. We become like the company we keep.

Sometimes I think about all the money I've spent on frivolous things. I consider how I could have given it to God-causes. Or how I could have blessed someone's life, abundantly. Or how I could have decreased our debt rather than adding to it.

The more we acquire, the less we give—and the less we get that inner satisfaction of rest and joy. Every decision includes a trade-off. A yes to one thing is a no to something else. Sometimes one yes can add three more things to your to-do list!

You trade one house for two—and now you're stressed out with maintenance, management, and making enough money to support the mortgage. You add more clothes to your closet—and now you have to spend an extra hour to keep that closet clean, plus there is more laundry to do.

More comes at a cost we usually cannot see. One thing impacts another.

For instance, you want a promotion so you can feel fulfilled. So you decide to work twelve-hour days, even though you are supposed to pick your kid up at 5:00. Because of your hard work, you do get the promotion. People clap. Everyone is happy for you. You did it. But now that you have it, you realize you aren't enjoying life anymore—or your family. When you pick up your child, you're usually late and in a bad mood. The daycare center is frustrated with you.

What you really wanted, you already had to begin with.

Many of us can't see how blessed and fulfilled we are *already.*

Then Jesus asked them, "When I sent you without purse, bag or sandals, did you lack anything?"

"Nothing," they answered. (Luke 22:35 NIV)

You can have *nothing* and still *have everything*. Many times, Jesus told His disciples not to worry about taking anything on their journey.

Take nothing for the journey—no staff, no bag, no bread, no money, no extra shirt. (9:3 NIV)

Carry no purse or bag or sandals. Do not greet anyone along the road. (10:4 BSB)

The less we have, the easier it is to go.

Another day, a man stopped Jesus and asked, "Teacher, what good thing must I do to get eternal life?" . . .

"If you want to **give it all you've got**," Jesus replied, "go sell your possessions; give everything to the poor. All your wealth will then be in heaven. Then come follow me." (Matt. 19:16, 21 MSG)

Essentially Jesus said to this man, "Give me all your soul is tied to. Untie yourself and follow me."

Crestfallen, the man walked away. He was holding on tight to a lot of things, things he couldn't bear to let go.

As he watched him go, Jesus told his disciples, "Do you have **any idea how difficult it is for the rich to enter God's king-**

dom? Let me tell you, it's easier to gallop a camel through a needle's eye than for the rich to enter God's kingdom."

The disciples were staggered. "Then who has any chance at all?"

Jesus looked hard at them and said, "No chance at all if you think you can pull it off yourself. **Every chance in the world if you trust God to do it.**" (vv. 23–26 MSG)

Friends, like this man, we are rich. It is not only the top 1 percent of Americans who are rich. "According to the Global Rich List, a $32,400 annual income will easily place American school teachers, registered nurses, and other modestly-salaried individuals, among the global 1% of earners."[1]

I say all this because I want you to know that Jesus is speaking to you too in this story. Likely, you're rich by the world's standard. But it is also important to know that Jesus is not necessarily addressing your wallet here as much as he is *your heart.*

Contentment is the ultimate rest. And reliance on Jesus is the place of greatest providence, no matter how much or little you have.

During this quarantine time, my family and I have fewer choices than ever. However, we also have joy and happiness like no other time. We've learned it isn't the trampoline park, restaurants, or mall that bring us joy, but the simple moments of being together. We already have it all.

What if what you think you need to have, *you already have* in Christ Jesus? What if you appreciated what you do have rather than what you don't? What if you made a conscious decision to decide what you own is good enough? To give thanks.

The issue with this man was not physical pieces of paper called money, the fabric that made up his fine clothes, or the gold that may have sat in his house. His issue was his soul-tie to stuff. Because of this, he walked away from following Jesus.

How often do we walk away when Jesus has all we need? And all the while, we think happiness and joy is somewhere else.

Let's Talk about Money

God never said, "Money is bad." Nor does He shame us for owning it, for happening upon it, or for earning it.

Some of us are financially blessed; we don't have to hate ourselves because of it. Some of us may be called to live in high-end neighborhoods or to a job where we can earn a lot of money. God uses people of wealth to give—to build orphanages, to start campaigns that reach nations, and to pay for programs for the down and out. God uses money to His end; He reaches people through it. He sends it forth as outreach. He uses living rooms for sweet hospitality. Everything belongs to the Lord, including every dollar bill in our checking account.

"The earth is the Lord's, and everything in it" (Ps. 24:1). God portions as He determines. "The blessing of the Lord makes a person rich, and he adds no sorrow with it" (Prov. 10:22).

"But to each one of us grace has been given as Christ apportioned it" (Eph. 4:7 NIV). Just as God rightly gives us grace to manage growth and money, He also gives us grace to be generous. I believe God gives us unique callings as it pertains to our money and gifts. As some have said, "We truly are blessed to be a blessing." Wisdom is uncovering how God wants us to use His resources—and then following through immediately.

When the love of God compels us to give, no greater joy fills us. When the love of God compels us to give up things, God in His grace gives us everything back in spades. This is the restful joy of following Jesus.

What gets in the way of this is when *what we own* validates us more than *who God says we are.*

Remember:

Only Christ makes us significant.

Only He can declare us worthy, validated, and good.

Only He is the rock we can firmly rely on.

Trust in stuff and expect stuff to save you. Or trust in God to see Him save you (Ps. 37:40). You choose.

Don't love the world's ways. Don't love the world's goods. Love of the world squeezes out love for the Father. Practically everything that goes on in the world—wanting your own way, wanting everything for yourself, wanting to appear important— has nothing to do with the Father. It just isolates you from him. The world and all its wanting, wanting, wanting is on the way out—but whoever does what God wants is set for eternity. (1 John 2:15–17 MSG)

Attachment to God or attachment to things. Wanting God or wanting what everyone else has. What have you chosen?

Consider yourself for a moment. Maybe you have an attachment to or a love of a car, a ministry, household goods, a certain destiny, prestige, power, notoriety, or something else.

Do you feel you can walk with a little more spring in your step or stand a bit higher because of these things? Do they prevent you from feeling weak or insecure? Do you feel better when:

- People think better about you?
- You appear more powerful?
- You have earned status?
- You think *I've made it*?
- You have achieved accomplishment and merit before others?
- Others speak highly about you?
- You feel above others?

With consumerism all around us, and a constant barrage of advertising coming at us, the world makes loud declarations about possessions. Then, after we buy, it is as if our stuff still speaks, saying, "Look at you now!" "You've really made it." "You are important now." And sometimes we agree with our stuff.

Yet Jesus speaks to us as He did to the rich man, saying, "Come, follow me" (Matt. 19:21). Can we hear Him enough

150

to set all our *things* down? Can we hear Him above the noise around us?

> Don't be obsessed with getting more material things. Be relaxed with what you have. Since God assured us, "I'll never let you down, never walk off and leave you," we can boldly quote,
>
>> God is there, ready to help;
>> I'm fearless no matter what.
>> Who or what can get to me? (Heb. 13:5–6 MSG)

The Real and Present Blessing Available

Currently, I have less—a smaller house, less stuff to organize, fewer bills, a shorter distance to travel to school, fewer activities to send my kids to—but I have more rest. I have more time with God. I have more space on my table to do things I love. I have more freedom to address my feelings of inadequacy, uncertainty, and distrust with God.

I have more time to know who my kids really are. And to be with God. It feels easier. Natural. More seamless.

> A devout life does bring wealth, but it's the **rich simplicity of being yourself before God**. (1 Tim. 6:6 MSG)

The greatest wealth I have is the simplicity of being myself, with God. This is not to say I won't someday have more. Or that God won't call me to get "stuff." His ways are not my ways. But what I do know is that right now, in this season, the way of less is *more*. I can enjoy small things I love.

Like looking out my window from my room and seeing grain wave in the distance. The smiles on my kids' faces. Dances at night. Walks in the day. God's heart for me in the sun. Popcorn in the afternoons. Freedom to spend extra money here or there. Giving that makes people smile. Time to spend journaling. And attention to storing up a treasure, where it lasts forever and ever and ever, in heaven. Amen.

In this place of less, what surfaces is a "knowing" of the nearness of God, the discovery of me, and the presence of those I love. Somehow, with my "stuff" removed, He feels closer.

I'm just as happy with little as with much, with much as with little. I've found the recipe for being happy whether full or hungry, hands full or hands empty.

Whatever I have, wherever I am, I can make it through anything in the One **who makes me who I am**. (Phil. 4:12–13 MSG)

I have all I need. And this feels good. It feels like rest.

prayer

Father, in You I trust. Forgive me for putting trust in lesser things. For looking to other "stuff" to provide me security, significance, or safety. I am guilty of putting these things before my love for You. I confess that I do not want to do this. I ask You to break every tie I have with "things," with "more," or with what I have "gained" so that I may follow You. I do not want to be enslaved to what is not supposed to own me. Give me the grace to do this and the help I need to change. You are my way, my truth, and my only source of life. In You alone I trust. In Jesus's name. Amen.

Receiving God's Love

One of the most integral pieces to releasing attachments to stuff is knowing God's love. To know you are loved is to be untouchable, immovable, and unbelievably sure of who you are, how to go forth, and what *not* to care about.

Paul prayed that the Ephesians would have a revelation of love:

> I pray that from his glorious, unlimited resources he will empower you with inner strength through his Spirit. Then Christ will make his home in your hearts as you trust in him. Your roots will grow down into God's love and keep you strong. And may you have the power to understand, as all God's people should, how wide, how long, how high, and how deep his love is. May you experience the love of Christ, though it is too great to understand fully. Then you will be made complete with all the fullness of life and power that comes from God. (Eph. 3:16–19)

I want less stuff and more of the fullness, life, and power that comes from God, don't you?

How to Begin to Receive God's Love

1. Ask the Holy Spirit to fill and empower your heart.

2. Ask for the strength, power, and experiential knowledge of God's love.

3. Continually dwell on the fact that, in Christ, nothing can separate you from His love (Rom. 8:38–39).

4. Notice what God is saying between the lines of your life, between the paragraphs of your prayer, and as you walk through your day.

God is speaking love to you. Will you notice it?

For God does speak—now one way, now another—though no one perceives it. (Job 33:14 NIV)

TEN

the way of words

REFRESH YOUR SOUL

The words we speak determine the life we live. They also impact the lives of those around us.

IKEA, the furniture store, recently conducted a classic experiment. For thirty days, one potted plant received criticism, insults, and mean words, while another plant received compliments and uplifting words. Both received equal water and light.

Guess which fared better?

After thirty days, the encouraged and uplifted plant was not only perkier but was thriving. The ridiculed one? It ended up "wilted and droopy."[1]

Our words can kill. Why? The "tongue has *the power* of life and death" (Prov. 18:21 NIV). The tongue—our words—hold literal power.

Can you remember negative words spoken over you? Perhaps when you were a kid, a friend or family member called you stupid, ugly, fat, or worthless. You probably held on to those words for a long time. How have these words lasted in your life? Taken ownership of you?

Words have staying power. Especially negative words. We feel them deeply. What our brains feel deeply, we remember increasingly.

Be careful, little mouth, what you say.

How do you speak?

My friend, you have the power of life and death in that mouth. You have the power to lift up or to tear down. You have the power to add to or steal joy.

Words are not just words.

After learning about the IKEA experiment, I thought it would be a good exercise to teach my kids about the power of words, plus I really wanted to test this experiment myself to see if it worked. And, equally important, I wanted to see the impact it would have on my kids. Outside of our house were two plants. I told my kids to talk nice to one and mean to the other.

So, to one of them, they whispered, "You're sweet. We love you. You're special."

To the other, they said, "We hate you. You're bad. We don't like who you are."

Guess what happened? After just a couple of days, the affirmed one grew three flowers and stood tall. The one they verbally ripped to shreds was downcast, droopy, and wilted.

Not only that, but my six-year-old daughter then decided to step on it.

Isn't it interesting that her mean words caused her to also take mean action? What we speak, we'll act on before long. Bad thoughts about a person soon become gossip. No restraint on what you hate becomes complaint. Inner anguish, without control, becomes destructive, angry outbursts.

Our future, our lives, and our circumstances are created through our words. This is biblical. Our words have the power to be healing or hurting, loving or hating, saving or killing, creating or destroying.

God created the whole world with words.
> By faith we understand that the universe was formed at God's command, so that what is seen was not made out of what was visible. (Heb. 11:3 NIV)

Salvation comes to life through words spoken from the heart.
> If you declare with your mouth, "Jesus is Lord," and believe in your heart that God raised him from the dead, you will be saved. (Rom. 10:9 NIV)

Jesus healed with just a word.
> The centurion replied, "Lord, I do not deserve to have you come under my roof. But just say the word, and my servant will be healed." (Matt. 8:8 NIV)

Our words can start fires—or put them out.
> It only takes a spark, remember, to set off a forest fire. A careless or wrongly placed word out of your mouth can do that. By our speech we can ruin the

world, turn harmony to chaos, throw mud on a reputation, send the whole world up in smoke and go up in smoke with it, smoke right from the pit of hell. (James 3:5–6 MSG)

How often do you consider what you speak?

Evaluate Your Words

If you say to someone, "You look so nice," and then critically look them up and down, where is your heart? If you say, "I'm fine," and then grunt and moan as you clean the kitchen, where is your heart?

If you say, "I don't care," and then talk about it behind your friend's back, where is your heart? If you say, "Your house is so nice, but it must be a bear to clean those five bathrooms," where is your heart?

Words of insecurity and condemnation—if they live in our heart—will sneak out of our mouth if we are not careful.

Some of this happened to me recently. I had a very heated discussion with my husband. In the midst of the argument and in the heat of the moment, I spoke death to him. I spoke words of accusation, blame, critique, fault-finding, and just general meanness. Why? Because I needed "to be heard." I needed "to defend myself." He "needed to know the truth."

Anyway, suffice it to say I got things off my chest—only to suffer later as my very own words came back around to hit me. *Look at what you are saying. You hypocrite. You're just as bad.* Ever felt convicted this way?

What do you let out of your mouth?

- I'll never be ___.
- Things will always be so ___.
- I don't know if God will ___.
- I am afraid that ___.
- I am so upset that ___ never happened.
- It will never be ___.
- I am furious that ___.
- I can't believe they ___.
- I am so irritated that ___.
- I don't have any chance of ___.
- I am not happy that ___.

Words are not just words.

It is not only said that "everyone will have to give account on the day of judgment for every empty word they have spoken" (Matt. 12:36 NIV) but also, "by your words you will be justified, and by your words you will be condemned" (v. 37 ESV).

What sits heavy on me today:

1. I am responsible for my every word.
2. When I speak, God *is* listening.
3. My words convict me in heaven and on earth.

God, help me. My words are powerful, and so are yours.

A Testimony

One group of people, against all odds, were amazingly and incredibly set free. The Israelites. For them, God did the unthinkable. He delivered them out of enslavement, He got them past enemy forces ready to annihilate them, He parted a sea, He gave them signs by day and wonders by night, and He miraculously fed them manna and provided water in the desert.

With the promised land ahead, life should have looked good. Except there was one problem: their words. They had a griping issue, a whining problem—mouths of negativity.

> They balked. "Why did you bring us out here to die in the wilderness? Weren't there enough graves for us in Egypt?" (Exod. 14:11)
>
> They grumbled. "What are we going to drink?" (15:24)
>
> They complained. "If only we had died by the LORD's hand in Egypt . . . but you have brought us out into this desert to starve this entire assembly to death." (16:3 NIV)
>
> They fought. "So they quarreled with Moses." (17:2 NIV)

Rather than speaking about what they did have, they homed in on what they didn't have. "If only we had died in Egypt! . . . Wouldn't it be better for us to go back to Egypt?" (Num. 14:2–3 NIV). And they said to each other, "Let's choose a new leader and go back to Egypt!" (4:4).

Instead of seizing freedom, they let their words lead them back to enslavement.

Later, when Caleb and the other eleven spies went into the promised land to scope things out, they came back and reported that "the people living there are *powerful*" (Num. 13:28). Caleb then said, "Let's go at once to take the land. . . . We can certainly conquer it!" (v. 30).

Yet what did the other spies do?

> They spread this bad report about the land among the Israelites: "The land we traveled through and explored will devour anyone who goes to live there. All the people we saw were huge. We even saw giants there, the descendants of Anak. Next to them we felt like grasshoppers, and that's what they thought, too!" (vv. 32–33)

Caleb never mentioned giants. Negativity and gossip make molehill-sized issues into monstrous mountains, every time. Secondhand talk expands the size of the problem. The more the information is discussed, the bigger it gets. Suddenly the Israelites were facing a fierce enemy that they could never, ever defeat. "Turn back, before we get hurt! We can't trust God now. Run!"

Their spoken unbelief became defeat. Because of all this, the Lord declared,

> But as surely as I live, and as surely as the earth is filled with the LORD's glory, not one of these people will ever enter that land. They have all seen my glorious presence and the miraculous signs I performed both in Egypt and in the wilderness, but again and again they have tested me by refusing to listen

to my voice. They will never even see the land I swore to give their ancestors. None of those who **treated me with contempt** will see it. (Num. 14:21–23)

It is unnerving to think that complaint can be contempt toward God.

A Different Spirit

At this time, God noted someone who was not like the others. God said, "My servant Caleb has a different spirit and follows me wholeheartedly," and therefore, He said, "I will bring him into the land he went to, and his descendants will inherit it" (Num. 14:24 NIV).

What was this different spirit? What was it that made this man unique and wholehearted? I want to learn a thing or two from him.

We can discover how to have this "different spirit" by considering how Caleb acted. Notice:

1. Caleb didn't allow other people's thoughts to hold him back. He agreed with God rather than dissenting and agreeing with other people's opinions.

   We have a "different spirit" when we agree *with* God rather than outside voices.

2. Caleb didn't fear being unlike everyone else, so he was blessed.

   We have a "different spirit" when we go God's way, even to the point of being misunderstood.

162

3. Caleb didn't whine, spread rumors, complain, or blow things out of proportion.

We have a "different spirit" when we see God's promises as bigger than any problem.

4. Caleb had faith that God would do it. He was ready to take the land when no one else was.

We have a "different spirit" when we walk "by faith, not by sight" (2 Cor. 5:7 ESV).

To be of this "different spirit" (imperfectly, I might add), I have begun to do a couple of things. First, I pause before I speak. A person of few words is not boring; they are wise. The less I say, the less I get in trouble. I ask myself:

Are my words truthful?
Are they needed?
Are they faith-building?

When I do this, I thrive. When I don't, I stir up issues or create an air that feels heavy and burdensome.

I repent immediately for wrong words. I pluck them out like a gray hair, the second I see them, and then I ask God to give me new vision for all that is going on around me. There is usually a better truth than the lie or the discouragement my mind wants to cling to. The Israelites were not far from their promised land; they were headed straight into it. We don't want to miss our best lands because we choose bad words.

Second, I upbuild my soul—and tell it what to do, like David did when he said, "Praise the LORD, my soul; all my inmost being, praise his holy name" (Ps. 103:1 NIV).

I boss my soul around and tell it to trust and obey God. I remind myself, often out loud:

The words of my prayers are effective to move mountains.

The words of my mouth reflect the meditations of my heart.

What I cannot fathom, God can do. It is not about my *understanding everything*; it is about my trusting Him.

Faith is not my doing; it is a gift from God. I can always ask for more of it.

God is at work, and He rewards me as I diligently seek Him.

When I ask for wisdom, God gives it to me.

As I walk in His light, I bring light.

Faith is my opportunity to see God move.

My faith does not depend on my human wisdom but on God's power.

I draw near to God with a sincere heart and the full assurance that His imparted faith brings.

The testing of my faith is building perseverance.

Third, I remind myself, through my words, that faith pleases God. And that faith takes risk. I speak my testimony instead of commiserating with stories of demise and fear.

The more I do this, the more my soul finds rest in the God who shows up, who never fails, and who is always with me. I start to feel on fire. I start to enjoy what He has called me to. I get eager to see Him show up. I expect good things.

To align my words with His Word is to allow streams of living water to flow. I do not partner with words that don't bring peace. I do not entertain gossip or complaint.

And therefore I stay full of life. I lay down in the promised land of His goodness. This keeps me in rest.

This is all available to you too.

prayer

God, my mouth is known to go before my head. I speak before I think. I call a friend before I have the wisdom to talk to You. I pour out my every emotion before I process what You would have me say. At times, I even blame, excuse, or rationalize my ways with my words. Even worse, I complain or gossip.

You know I am not perfect with my words. I ask You to help me with them. I don't want to speak what will be injurious to Your heart, my faith, or others. I want to cultivate good soil, so what You are doing may be watered and grown. My bad words often steal the good life You are growing, both in my life and the lives of others. Make me wise about my words. May my words bring life, peace, and hope more than they steal, kill, and destroy. Give me new faith that speaks volumes on faith and love. May my mouth be a releaser of divine words—everything You want said, through me.

Grant me the ability to be a peace-focused gatekeeper of my mouth for Your glory. In Jesus's name. Amen.

Good Gatekeepers

As you know, the power of life and death is in your tongue (Prov. 18:21). You have the ability to create life through your words, as you compliment someone or encourage them in who Christ created them to be, just as much as you have the ability to kill their worth by speaking teardowns and discouragement.

How will you speak? Will you be known for keeping your word, or will you be known as untrue to your word? Will you be honest, or a liar?

How to Keep Your Word

1. See it through: what you say you will, *do*.

2. Speak only the words you'd want their subject to hear.

3. Change the topic if you feel uncomfortable with the content.

4. Pause before you speak.

5. Pray before you complain.

6. Ponder God's plan before you say yes.

7. Avoid promising to do things your future self will hate.

8. Tell people you've promised to speak only what is good, not other stuff.

9. Reflect on what you have said at the end of each day. You can always apologize if you need to. This, again, brings life.

ELEVEN

the way of christ in us

BE LED TO GREATER THINGS

Simply Jesus.

Jesus saved and saves me.
Jesus loves me.
Jesus wants to be with me.
Jesus leads me.
Jesus forgives me.
For eternity.

Because of Jesus, I get rest when I can find none. Peace in the line of fire. Help when I haven't warranted it. Salvation—regardless of how I perform, how I look, what I've done, what people say, or how many friends or likes I have. None of it really matters.

Jesus gives me everything when I don't deserve anything. It is all because of Him and not even the smallest bit dependent on me.

It's kind of like going to a candy store, as a child, without money. Perhaps you just hope for a free jelly bean or something similar, but when you show up, the owner does something profound. He tells you to hold out your hand—but instead of one small piece of candy, he gives you the keys to the whole store. He gives you the thing he poured blood, sweat, and tears into. For free. Without you doing anything. It makes no sense. You didn't deserve it; he just gave it. Jesus gives you the whole kit and caboodle. Everything you don't deserve and more.

You do nothing except welcome Him inside your heart. And it pleases Him to do all this. His sacrifice is so immense—He turns every meaningful table to our advantage, stacks the decks in our favor, and wins eternity for us, even though we still make horrible mistakes right in His face.

Oh, the love of Jesus constantly chooses us! Remembering Jesus is continual rest for our souls. Jesus is Sabbath for our souls. "The Son of Man is Lord, even over the Sabbath" (Matt. 12:8).

What Jesus did is finalized and finished.

What Jesus paid for you is bought and secure forever.

What identity He gave you, you now habitually walk in.

You have been transferred from the kingdom of darkness into the kingdom of light. You no longer walk with a "sin nature"—you are a new creation.

You are empowered by the Holy Spirit.

When you confess Christ, sin has no access to your soul. And, best of all, Christ is alive in you. This means no depths of hell, no situation, no person, can ever separate you from the love of God. And if God is for you, and in you, who or what can be against you (Rom. 8:31)?

What if you really believed this? What if you let this become the reality you worked and lived by?

Receive the Sabbath rest the Lamb afforded you on the cross. Relish the new reality that forms, not only your identity, but your destiny.

You do not even belong to yourself anymore. (1 Pet. 2:9)

You are no longer possessed by yourself (your motives, willpower, or desires) but by God. (1 Pet. 2:9; Eph. 5:17–18)

You belong to Christ. (1 Cor. 3:23)

You are a chosen people . . . God's special possession. (1 Pet. 2:9)

Begin to understand the magnitude of this. There is an almost-absurd empowerment that lives in you.

It is not you.

It is not your work.

It is not your show.

It is the Holy Spirit.

You are now "dead to sin but alive to God" (Rom. 6:11 NIV). These are not pleasantries but *realities.* The amazing Almighty God lives *outward* from the temple *within you.*

Take a Sabbath rest, my soul. Jesus has done it and He will do it. We can trust Him through it.

> The Helper, the Holy Spirit, whom the Father will send in my name, he will teach you **all** things and bring to your remembrance **all** that I have said to you. (John 14:26 ESV)

What mental chatter matters when the mind of Christ is now ruling, teaching, and directing you? What is there left to accomplish—in your own strength—when the strength of God is moving within and through you?

Via submission and by the direction of the Holy Spirit, Jesus gives us permission to seize a lifestyle of rest rather than living bound by a lifetime of stress.

Refreshing the Temple

The Holy Spirit, who makes the things of the Father and the Son evident, lives in you. "Don't you realize that your body is the temple of the Holy Spirit?" (1 Cor. 6:19).

How would we treat a physical temple? Just as we wouldn't ignore out-of-place pews or a broken front door—or intruders who came into the building with the wrong motives—we must care for our temple. If we don't, we risk quenching God's Spirit and extinguishing the passion and fervor of love that wants to work out from within us.

I don't want to do this. We quench the Spirit when we live by fear or when we walk in timidity, uncertainty, or doubt. Confusion and disillusionment come with doubt. They convince us our mind is not sound. This is not of God.

For God has not given us a spirit of fear and timidity, but of **power, love,** and a **sound mind**. (2 Tim. 1:7)

A spirit at rest walks in the power of God. It is filled with the love of God. It is led by a sound and under-control mind.

You can tell if you are walking by the Spirit of God because your life will tend to be filled with God's power and affectionate love, and you'll have a calm and collected mind, not one driven by fear and timidity.

Do you walk filled by the Spirit, constantly in touch with the Sabbath rest of God?

I have noticed that when God fills me with love by the Spirit, it is not only to love others but also to love and care for myself. Receiving this care, for me, is part of receiving what God has for me. In this way, and in order to submit to the Spirit, I often choose to:

Feed myself right so I can think right.

Work out to gain strength to run my race of faith as well and as long as I can.

Lie down to recover when I feel tired.

Seek to honor my body's quiet requests, honoring the masterpiece God created it to be.

Care to take time to connect with the Holy Spirit by taking a walk, gardening, singing, dancing, painting, or whatever.

Break away to pray and listen.

Allow myself recovery time.

I've found the quenching of the Holy Spirit is not only a spiritual quenching but a physical one when I don't listen to my temple's prompting for inner care. If I overwork myself, I lose my sound-mind connection with God. If I overschedule my day, I start to feel powerless over it. If I try to be everything to everyone and don't sit down for a minute, I lose love.

I get frustrated more easily with people. I start downgrading my time with Jesus. I stop listening to the heartbeat of the Spirit, who wants to guide, instruct, counsel, and correct me. I get lost to confusion and disillusionment.

I live in unrest.

Led to Love, Joy, and Peace

But by the Spirit there is freedom.

> Now the Lord is the Spirit, and where the Spirit of the Lord is, there is liberty [emancipation from bondage, true freedom]. (2 Cor. 3:17 AMP)

Jesus illustrated freedom for us. Remember all the times Jesus pulled away from people to pray? Remember how He re-communed with friends over a bonfire on the shore? How He made time to attend a wedding?

These things are frivolous to some. But they are freedom and rejuvenation to those who walk by the Spirit.

Some of us have tired out our bodies. We've forgotten to sleep. We aren't eating right. We've forgotten to care for our temple. Friends, it is not selfishness to sit down. It is not indulgent to lie down. It is not wrong to take needed time with God. What good is an incapacitated person—a fearful, timid, and foggy-minded individual—to the work of God?

Jesus wasn't self-indulgent; He was practical.

When we care for our physical and emotional needs, we are also caring for our temple and our connection with the Holy Spirit. This prepares us for action.

Give yourself time for prayers like this one:

> I pray that out of his glorious riches he may strengthen [me] with power through his Spirit in [my] inner being, so that Christ may dwell in [my heart] through faith. (Eph. 3:16–17 NIV)

Don't worry about what you aren't doing on your own, for the Spirit will produce every good thing in you—everything you want to own.

> But the fruit of the Spirit is **love, joy, peace**, forbearance, kindness, goodness, faithfulness, gentleness and self-control. Against such things there is no law. (Gal. 5:22–23 NIV)

173

There is no law against rest. Rest makes the fruit of the Spirit ripe for the picking. When people get a taste of the sweetness and the goodness of God, they usually want to know more about it.

Led to Faith and Greater Works

Remember the wandering Israelites? God said the issue with them was that they did not "receive the promises with faith" (Heb. 4:2 MSG). He also tells us that if we believe, we can experience this state of resting.

> And so this **is still a live promise**. It wasn't canceled at the time of Joshua; otherwise, God wouldn't keep renewing the appointment for "today." The promise of "arrival" and "rest" is still there for God's people. God himself is at rest. And at the end of the journey we'll surely rest with God. So let's keep at it and eventually arrive at the place of rest, not drop out through some sort of disobedience. (vv. 8–11 MSG)

Via Christ in us, via the Holy Spirit, empowering rest—enduring rest—is here for us.

The key is believing and trusting God will act according to His Word.

Do you believe—I mean, *really* believe, truly believe—God's Word? Do you trust it like you own it? Like you *will* see it happen? Like it is going to happen as much as lunch will?

> Now faith is the assurance (title deed, confirmation) of things hoped for (divinely guaranteed), and the evidence of things

not seen [the conviction of their reality—faith comprehends as fact what cannot be experienced by the physical senses]. (11:1 AMP)

Apprehend by faith what you cannot see in reality.

Faith is often kept and kindled practically. We spend time with God even though we hear the bells of a thousand other to-do items ringing in our mind. We persist with singing a worship song at home even though our thoughts want to go ten other directions. We keep strong in the spirit even though our circumstances disagree with what God says. We hear people saying things, yet we still trust God.

In order to do the works of Christ, with the faith of Christ, we must live by the Spirit. We must abide.

Jesus knew how to abide. He abided with the Father.

Very truly I tell you, the Son can do nothing by himself; he can do only what he sees his Father doing, because whatever the Father does the Son also does. (John 5:19 NIV)

He also abided with the Spirit. R. A. Torrey, author, writer, evangelist, pastor, and educator, tells us Jesus

was "begotten of the Holy Spirit."

"offered Himself without spot to God through the working of the Holy Spirit."

was "anointed and fitted for service by the Holy Spirit."

was "led by the Holy Spirit in His movements here upon earth."

was "taught by the Spirit who rested upon Him."

"gave commandments unto His Apostles whom He had chosen through the Holy Spirit."

"wrought His miracles here on earth in the power of the Holy Spirit."

"by the power of the Holy Spirit [was] raised from the dead."[1]

If Jesus lived abiding, how much more do we need to rest with Christ, full of the Spirit and moving in faith?

Other things are vanity.

> Unless the LORD builds the house,
>   those who build it labor in vain. (Ps. 127:1 ESV)

Jesus abided and built an indestructible kingdom. He did great works. He achieved the inconceivable. What might happen if we were to lay down our agenda and actually become restored through Jesus and the Spirit? To allow His work *in* us to work *out* from us?

When we walk by the power of the Holy Spirit, God's horsepower often gets behind us. He does it so we don't have to. It gets a whole lot easier.

With less pressure, there is more rest.

Led to Safety

Always remember: no one can steal what Christ has paid for. No one can take the Spirit from us.

When we put our trust in Him, I like to think of it as if we take our trust out of ourselves and literally place it into *Christ*. All our hope and belief are now in God and His faithfulness. With this, we lean on Him to take care of us. We have faith in Him to lead us and help us. We allow ourselves to be "hidden in Christ" (Col. 3:3).

This is powerful because the Lord is "invincible in battle" (Ps. 24:8).

Do you see the beauty here? When you are hidden in Christ, you become hidden to enemy forces. The comments. The insults. The issues. The snarls. The effects of your day. *No.* They can't touch you; you are hidden away.

The enemy can't rob you of rest. He can't steal trust. He can't find you.

prayer

God, I want—no, I need—Your grace. You know and I know I'm not perfect. You know and I know it has to be You doing this stuff. You know and I know You are my only way.

So, God? I ask that You might give me the blessing of having Your favor upon me. I ask that You provide for me, lead me, equip me, empower me, teach me, and give me all the things I need to stay ever close to You. Make all these gifts known in my mind so that I might thank You and praise You in every way for what You have done.

And, until then, I'll thank You today, anyway. I thank You for keeping me, for holding me, and for securing me in Your love. I thank You for being the shepherd of my soul and the keeper of my life. I trust in You always. You, through Jesus, have already given me more than a girl's heart could ever ask for.

I am so grateful.

I keep going lower, and, as I do, I keep seeing You higher and higher—oh, this is favor and grace. For I am getting a glimpse of how much You're in charge; You love me and You want me. This is the ultimate rest, and I thank You for it. In Jesus's name. Amen.

How to Be Present with God

1. Invite God into everything.
   Your work. Your walk. Your ways.

2. Expect to see Him in the big and the little things.
   Look for Him, listen for Him, talk with Him, and wait for Him.

3. Observe God in your day; note what is good.
   Look for Him in nature. See Him in others. Observe what He is doing today. Take note of how you are feeling, and bring it to Him.

4. Vocally give thanks to God for what is good.

5. Ask God what He wants you to know.

6. Watch how God speaks through:
   - people
   - circumstances
   - His Word
   - an inner reply
   - nature

PART 3

---

set boundaries

Wisdom pursues God's highest good over what appears good in the moment. It doesn't react now; it trusts God's appointed time. It doesn't force itself to be everything to everyone; it remembers who it is in Christ.

Wisdom takes action on what's most important before lesser things take advantage of the delay. It writes occasions on the calendar, months in advance, so good things don't creep over greater moments, memories, missions, and milestone break-throughs. Wisdom keeps watch for what matters and guards these things like a hawk.

What matters to you? Loving your family? Enhancing your marriage? Spending time with God? Receiving His love? Handing it out? Giving yourself unto a cause God is leading you into?

Hopefully, at the top of your list is love.

> And now these three remain: faith, hope and **love**. But the greatest of these is **love**. (1 Cor. 13:13 NIV)

> Do everything with **love**. (16:14)

> If I speak in the tongues of men or of angels, but do not have **love**, I am only a resounding gong or a clanging cymbal. If I have the gift of prophecy and can fathom all mysteries and all knowledge, and if I have a faith that can move mountains, but do not have **love**, I am nothing. If I give all I possess to the poor and give over my body to hardship that I may boast, but do not have **love**, I gain nothing. (13:1–3 NIV)

If you aren't loving, why are you doing it, anyway?

Without love, obligations and duties leave us full of regrets and remorse. Without faith and hope, we return to the starting line again: defeated and searching for our lost rest. We become a doormat. We get walked upon, and we feel used. We lose ground. We lose faith.

Only *real* love, coupled with faith and hope, makes us on fire, unstoppable, called, purposeful, and on-mission. Like nothing can stop us. Like nothing can tear us down or break us.

I want to live from that—don't you? But how? How do we preserve *real* love so we aren't unnerved by the million needs around us?

We set up boundaries.

Boundaries are borders. They help us see the valuable and ditch the peripheral. They keep in what matters and let out what doesn't. They preserve simplicity and prevent complexities from taking advantage of us.

To get more practical, boundaries are like the margins on this page. They offer whitespace. With boundaries we have room to think before reacting. They protect the integrity of the story.

Without margins, mumbo-jumbo or ran dom drawings could get written all over your pages. I could take red and black markers and scribble-scrabble all over your story. I could violate the space—and make your main message unreadable. Your purpose and emphasis could get lost. I could take away value from you—just because you let me.

Boundaries are smart borders around your story. They help you to say, "No. I don't want you to draw on my page, please." They let people know you mean it.

Whether they intend to or not, people, circumstances, and expectations can steal things from us if we let them. They can talk over us, redirect us, demand from us, hurt us, or keep us busy, if we are not careful. This is why we must vehemently fight to keep the scribbles off our pages in order to preserve pure love.

Friends, I don't know if you've realized it yet, but this part of the book is mission-critical for you. It is absolutely invaluable for both obtaining rest and maintaining it. It requires courage. You will have to change things. You will have to think hard. It is not something that happens by default.

The habits you create today will create a more restful tomorrow. It's that simple. And the more you learn to love, the more you can be sure you are investing in the one thing that lasts into eternity. This sounds like a calling worthy of attention, doesn't it?

Thoughtfully discern, with God, where, how, and why you need boundaries. And practically and tactically implement these borders with determination to see them through.

You have come this far. You can do this. Rest is tangible. Don't give up now. I believe your life is about to be radically changed.

TWELVE

what boundaries are and are not

Not too long ago, I was at a tennis court. A woman on the court next to me approached me with a military air. She demanded I go over and inform a group of men they shouldn't act a certain way on the tennis court and that they should leave. She was so declarative about what I *needed* to do that I felt like saluting her and replying, "Yes, ma'am!"

I was a little scared of her, I'll admit. I felt obligated to join her cause against these men, whatever it was. She also worked at the tennis courts, which complicated matters a bit.

Because of the "authority" she carried, as a good girl I wanted to make her happy. But I had been learning from my past interactions—all the times when I'd automatically said yes—and I decided to go a new way. I replied to her, "No, thanks. I am not interested in getting into this today."

I didn't feel I had to give her a hundred reasons why I wouldn't do it. I didn't have to appease her or be concerned about what she might think of me.

I just chose to say no.

One reason was I thought about my future self. If I listened to this woman, I knew I'd probably later hate myself for it. She'd already acted heated with these men, and action on my part would have inserted me right into the middle of a conflict that had nothing to do with me. With tensions already high, adding my voice to the problem was bound to have neither a godly nor good effect. The situation probably would have blown up.

Plus, my thoughts about "the tennis incident" wouldn't have ended on that court. Undoubtedly, I'd go home thinking about how I acted, how I could have done better, and how I should have said no. I would think all night about how I yelled and also how I took it out on my family later. I'd be repenting all night long. I know how this goes . . . I've been on this carousel before. *No*, I decided, right then and there. *This situation is not my burden to carry.*

Boundaries are a tool to help your future self. This way you don't trigger, blow up, act out, retaliate, burn out, passive-aggressively insult someone, or create a greater mess.

On that tennis court, I used holy discernment so I didn't involve myself in a matter I didn't belong in. It's as if I could hear Jesus saying, *No. No. No. Do all things in love, Kelly.*

To have acted otherwise would have been to appease a demanding woman. Even if I convinced myself it was in love, that would be a lie. Helping this woman would not have been motivated by love. Or service. It would have been sourced from fear. *I need to help. I have to act. What will she think of me? I want to avoid awkwardness with her. I need to be helpful. I can fix things.*

Where is your work sourced from? Fear or love? Faith or obligation? Hope or the hopeless sense you have to rescue others or come to their aid?

What Boundaries Are Not

Our highest calling is love. To love and to be loved.

With this, it is important to understand what boundaries are not. They are not an "out"—out of loving.

And if I have the gift of prophecy [and speak a new message from God to the people], and understand all mysteries, and [possess] all knowledge; and if I have all [sufficient] faith so that I can remove mountains, but do not have love [reaching out to others], I am nothing. (1 Cor. 13:2 AMP)

Boundaries are all about love. They are not *walls*. They are not meant to be used in retaliation, to punish bad behavior, or to change someone's actions. They are not excuses to rationalize running away from others because you fear you can't love them. They are not for avoiding patience or evangelism. They are not an escape. They are not naming people *toxic* or *bad* and running away. They are not paranoia that people are taking advantage of you.

The goal of boundaries is to create a reserve *of love* so you observe the calling *to* love.

Anytime you step back, it is always with the goal of stepping closer to something greater: love. This may mean you draw back as you think about what to say, then move in to speak intentional truth. Or you pull back to pray and gain wisdom on what to do, then, when the season is right, meet together. Either way, margins are meant to preserve your heart in all things. In this, you won't be reactive to comments, triggers, or happenings; you will be ready. You will have a plan. You will operate in purer love. Beyond this, boundaries should:

Position you to love with greater capacity.

Help you stay close to what you love.

Aid you in communicating effectively.

Provide focus on what matters most.

Remove stumbling blocks that may cause sin.

Increase joy, meaning, and connectedness.

Reduce stress, nervousness, and fear.

Build stronger relationships.

Increase faith and your emotional well-being.

All this gives your mind more room to relax. To have a plan is to plan for rest and connection. To have more time to sit in the love of God is to walk full of His peace that touches others. To find more life and power in Him is to gain new strength for all that is ahead.

> I pray that from his glorious, unlimited resources he will **empower you with inner strength** through his Spirit. Then Christ will make his home in your hearts as you trust in him. Your roots will grow down into God's love and **keep you strong**. And may you have the power to understand, as all God's people should, how wide, how long, how high, and how deep his love is. May you **experience the love of Christ**, though it is too great to understand fully. Then you will be made complete with all the **fullness of life and power that comes from God**. (Eph. 3:16–19)

It is hard to burst forth with God's life and power if you haven't first received His love and strength. If you haven't, you'll strive for love from others rather than living from God's. Boundaries keep your heart pure and able to love others from God's bounty rather than with your scraps. This way, you don't have to be afraid of how others may react, what they will say, or how you will handle things. You know the bounds, and within those bounds you can love with abandon.

Are you beginning to see how powerful boundaries can be?

Stepping Out in Boundaries

I don't know about you, but I can easily ask myself:

If I say no, what will they think of me?
If I can't help, can they really handle it?

If I don't participate, will they forget about me?
If I am unable to help, will they talk about me?
If I keep space for myself, am I selfish?
If I don't do this, who will?

Or I say to myself:

The guilt of not doing this is going to kill me.
If I say no someone else will do it, even better than I would,
    and I won't matter anymore.
I can't let people down.
I am a bad Christian for not helping.

Say I meet a negative complainer at a party. I may have the opportunity to move away from them, but I am afraid of cutting them off or hurting their feelings. So, rather than politely excusing myself after three minutes, I stay for an hour. Then, after feeling no better for having the conversation, I hate myself for it. And I hate how I didn't talk with my friend whom I hadn't seen for years.

It is easy to get sucked in. Why? Because without boundary lines, we become wishy-washy. Pressure and obligation force us into a caretaking role where we feel responsible for other people's feelings, their expectations, and the sum of their emotional well-being.

In truth, we are not responsible. The second we allow this dynamic to happen, we cultivate complexity over simplicity. This impacts us spiritually, emotionally, and often physically.

We didn't allow for margin. We got sucked in. Trapped in someone else's world, not the one Christ calls us to.

Now, I understand excusing ourselves can feel awkward, uncomfortable, or even rude. We get concerned with the message we're sending and how people will take it. But maybe the person on the other side needs "the message."

Regardless, their response is not our business. Our business is making sure we walk in what God has for us.

Peter did just this. When the disciples saw Jesus walking on the lake, Peter courageously asked, "Lord . . . tell me to come to you" (Matt. 14:28).

Jesus replied, "Yes, come" (v. 29).

Peter stepped out of the boat and—for a bit—walked on water!

Can you imagine the faith boost this was? How life changing it would be? How wonderful to participate with Jesus like this?

But what if Peter never took that opportunity? What if instead he got caught up in how he looked to the other disciples? *Will I seem too presumptuous or arrogant?*

Faith always looks like *something*. There are times it may look like disappointing others. There are other times it may look like not loving others, even though you very well may be. There are days when people may talk about you behind your back because of your faith. This doesn't mean you aren't doing things right.

Do not allow people's opinions and proclamations to hinder what God is doing. He could be working a miracle in your life. What looks like indulgence to some is God's incredible breakthrough for another. Jesus had critics too; He didn't let them stop Him. Ultimately, He defeated the grave through resurrection life power. No one is laughing and shaming Him now. Or, at least, I am not.

People may not agree with you. They may not like what you have to say. It may even feel horrifying to you. But in the end, preserve God's greater story. Choose courage and risk. Believe you are walking with Jesus. He will give you strength. Stand up for your future, your family, and your faith.

What Is Imperative

Every choice to do something is also a choice *not* to do something else. Your yes to going on a girls' trip may also be saying no to attending your daughter's recital. Or your yes to a role at church may mean saying no to that weekend hour you have to sit down to read God's Word. Saying yes to a phone call may mean missing the walk you had been looking forward to for a week.

Rest-filled people know how to say no. They remember what is *most important*, so they don't accidentally welcome confusion and complexity into their lives.

Do you know how to say no to what you can't handle? To burdens that are not yours to carry? To a project that actually does not fall within your role? To people who are well-meaning but expect too much?

This can be one of the hardest areas of life to conquer. Self-will and sturdy resolve are required. You may have to endure feeling "a little bad." But don't give up. This is normal.

You can say no. Just like this:

Nope. Not now. I can't. I am unable to. Thank you, but
no.

I appreciate that you thought of me regarding _____, but
at this time _____.

While I would love to say yes, unfortunately due to _____,
I have to say no.

I will be able to help you (insert date when this is
feasible).

No, not at this time, but I so value the heart you are putting behind this.

I am crazy excited about what you are doing, and I can
get behind it in the following ways: _____.

While I'd love to go full-force into this, my family needs
me right now.

No. However, here are some other people or resources
that may be able to help you.

Please circle back (insert time frame), and perhaps I will
have more availability then.

I am happy to help you, but please note: I am only going
to be able to do _____ and _____.

I've found that after I say no often comes the question, Why?

Why not?

Why can't you?

Why? What if we had you do it like this?

Why? It only requires that you ____.

Understand: you never *have to* answer these questions. You also don't have to defend your decision. You have the ability to say, "I really am grateful for the opportunity, I am just unable to at this point."

You can do this with peace and love in your heart. Saying no doesn't mean you are bad, nor does it mean you are selfish. It means you are seeking to preserve good things, like time, space, vision, family hours, and God-opportunity. Your highest pursuits. Love that lasts.

Trust your good decision. Envision the better outcome. Give thanks to the Holy Spirit for leading you. Give praise for the time, the relationships, or the calling you have preserved. You can't do it all, after all.

Trust your prayerful decision, by faith. Be decisive and single-minded. Remember that your goal is to preserve the purity of your heart, peace, and abounding love. Stand firm. Keep faith.

But he who is uncertain [about eating a particular thing] is condemned if he eats, because he is not **acting** from faith. Whatever is not from faith is sin [whatever is done with doubt is sinful]. (Rom. 14:23 AMP)

prayer

God, give me the heart to care about Your cares first. Sometimes I don't know what this looks like because other stuff comes on me. Show me what to take off: what to delegate, what to ask for help with, what to let go of, what to say goodbye to. Show me how to obey You, first and foremost. I want You above all else. I want my heart to be pure. I want to be real with You and to really know You. In Jesus's name. Amen.

What to Do If You Are Experiencing Abuse

My friend and pastoral counselor Karen Mortensen offers wise counsel on this topic. In her words:

My office is often occupied with women in abusive relationships who have been told to remain in them.

Horrifically, I have known women to commit suicide because they thought they had no other choice. I have seen women beaten and defeated in body and spirit because they believed there was no place for them to turn!

Physical and emotional abuse cross every boundary God has established.

People who abuse are loved powerfully by God, but they live as we all do with free choice. They have chosen poorly. Abusers need to know that their actions have dire consequences. Abuse steals and crushes self-image. So often, the husband's abuse creates the feeling that God has abandoned the wife. Her self-image is ravished.

If God can do a miracle, He can do it at a safe distance. God is a life preserver, and emotional death is so hard to recover from.

In my mind, the minute a man abuses his wife, he has broken the marital covenant.

My advice is always to stay safe and maintain your boundaries. If you are living with an abuser, move to a safe place and pray. God will guide your next steps. This is so important to me; I have seen tragedies because women could not bring themselves to leave an abuser. It brings me to tears.

THIRTEEN

the heart of boundaries

M y friend texted me:

Hey there, I am struggling; can you call me? I
need prayer.

I need to be there for her, I thought. *She needs help. God may
use me here.*

Not without hesitation, I laid down my time with God,
picked up the phone, and called her. But I had only a little
time, and she had *much* to say. I wanted to rush her along, so
my words became forced and unhelpful. I needed to get out
the door to pick up my kids from school. *Why did I even pick
up the phone? I need to wrap up this call.* Not knowing how else
to get rid of her, I barked out instructions and fix-it schemes.

I told her, "You should . . . It is really about this . . . Go and do this . . ."

Later I felt horrible about how obnoxiously prescriptive I was. In fact, all night long, I kept thinking of how I failed her. I wanted to leave "I'm sorry" messages on her voicemail, but I didn't want to drag her down again. I'd acted like a jerk, just throwing action items in her face—so now she had more to deal with than before. All she'd needed was for someone to listen.

Why did I even pick up the phone to begin with? I knew how little time I had and what her needs would likely be. But still . . . I felt *obligated.*

I suppose I wanted her to like me even more. I wanted to be valuable. I wanted to preserve my "savior" position.

Do you ever do things like this too?

- Do you try to win favor with others?
- Do you feel like a doer, a "savior," or an over-helper? (Perhaps clean the kids' rooms when they're capable of doing it themselves?)
- Do you seek to gain people's approval? Or to keep a perceived position?
- Do you manage others' emotions?
- Do you want an outcome more than the process of working things out?
- Perhaps you aim to keep your favored position: best employee, loved daughter, precious friend, or feeling first in God's eyes?

Jesus did not fight to keep the position of rich and prestigious king; He came as a human servant, leaving the abundance of heaven for our grime. And by taking this low position He solidified our position within His eternal love.

Authentic ministry lets go of position-seeking and self-gain for enduring love.

Otherwise, the in-laws want us over five times a week. The boss wants us to work sixty-hour weeks. The needy friend wants us over three times a week for her emotional breakdowns. The teacher wants us to come in for reading hour every day. The out-of-town friend wants us to meet up with her every week, even though we live two hours away.

If we do these things for them, we resent them later. Or we get upset because they take us for granted and don't realize how much we do. And now we've lost all our precious time.

And we knew we shouldn't have done it to begin with. We think, *People always take advantage of me.*

Our original intent—to love—was right, but the ultimate result is wrong. We snap. We dislike them. We talk behind their back. This is not love. Later, we find ourselves acting out through pity parties, passive-aggressiveness, irritation, gossip, resentment, or a victim mindset.

Always reflect before responding yes or no to someone. Give yourself a timeout to *think, pray,* and *ask.* Consider how it will affect you in the future.

Ask yourself before saying yes, *Am I working for a favored position, or am I aiming to* really *love? Am I wanting to feel wanted, or am I wanting to do this unto the Lord? Am I going to pay the price for this decision later, or is God leading me to do this?*

Am I now trying to win the favor and approval of men, or of God? Or am I seeking to please someone? If I were still trying to be popular with men, I would not be a bond-servant of Christ. (Gal. 1:10 AMP)

I had to face the fact that my call with my friend wasn't done out of love or out of ministry unto Jesus; it was done *unto me*, so I could feel important, necessary, and helpful.

When we do things unto ourselves, we want rewards for self. Here, we are outcome-based versus love-based. We expect one thing to lead to another.

I control her to meet my emotional needs.

I use manipulation to get what I really want.

I am fearful, so I want to make sure things work out my way.

I coerce him to agree with me so I feel good.

I hate myself because I gave in, thinking this will help me not act this way again.

I feel embarrassed and then try to make up for it by how I act with her.

I resent him because I can't live the life I want to lead, and then I get upset.

Which of these do you do?

Do nothing out of selfish ambition or vain conceit. Rather, in humility value others above yourselves. (Phil. 2:3 NIV)

Making Heart-Room for God's Move

If you keep yourself pure, you will be a special utensil for honorable use. Your life will be clean, and you will be ready for the Master to use you for every good work. (2 Tim. 2:21)

To have boundaries is to preserve mental space, time, and bandwidth for God's special assignments. God may call you at any given moment for any given thing. Are you available? If you have one thousand things lined up in a day, with all your mental chatter about what you have to do and what people need, you will likely not hear God's calling.

God searches for those who are ready and committed. "For the eyes of the LORD range throughout the earth to strengthen those whose hearts are fully committed to him" (2 Chron. 16:9 NIV).

I want God to see me, ready and available. I want Him to strengthen me. I want to be so ready for God's good work, His callings, and His giftings that His good comes my way. Don't you?

Boundaries discard distractions so we can place our attention on God. Peace increases as we follow Jesus, the "Prince of Peace" (Isa. 9:6).

How can we do this?

If you are meeting with the friend who always brings you stress, consider, *Should I meet with her again today? Maybe getting together after her workday is done is not the best idea. Meeting on the weekend may work better for me to minister to her heart, instead.*

Or if someone is demanding a decision and you don't have peace about it, consider, *I need more time to decide.* Be okay with telling them you need more time. Take time to pray.

After prayer, you may find that God leads you to unusual answers for your typical problems. He may lead you to bring another friend with you when you meet that stressed-out friend. Or He may give you a key piece of information for that decision you would not have had if you immediately said yes. Keep faith in boundaries. Be decisive. Follow peace.

My husband and I have boundaries in our marriage. One of them is that I do not accept friend requests on Facebook from past boyfriends. This may not feel peaceful in the present moment. However, it preserves future peace and prevents potential future problems. We also don't personally message someone of the opposite sex without each other knowing about it. Again, we follow the Prince of Peace, keeping in mind future peace.

We should always consider our future.

Boundaries clear a highway for the Lord's showing up. They ready us for His best work as we preserve the pureness of our heart and keep our deep attention on Him.

> In the wilderness **prepare**
> **the way** for the LORD;
> make straight in the desert
> a highway for our God. (Isa. 40:3)

What if our every relationship, every decision, every action, and every conversation could become a highway, set apart, for the Lord's showing up?

What Your Heart Needs

Do you have needs? Many days, I forget I have them. Because everyone else needs so much of me, I figure I'm just there to meet their every need. I lose track of me.

But when I make time to worship and praise God, I remember some things. Things like: at the foot of the cross, I am the same as the drug addict desperately pursuing Jesus and equal to the politician who needs a Savior. I am just like the sexual sinner who is coming to see the error of her ways. I need the Shepherd's care too.

Here I can see it is not selfish to need help or rest or downtime with God; I am human. I am not "out for number one" because I take time to work out; I am in need of energy and a highly functional body to keep me going forward. I am not bad; I am aware that my body is a temple (1 Cor. 6:19).

Being honest about my needs helps me to love others, instead of feeling like everything I do is forced labor. After all, "[I am] no longer a slave but God's own child" (Gal. 4:7).

I am God's child. Children have needs. They ask for help. They accept care. They aren't bad because they have needs.

It is okay that you and I have needs. We don't have to feel bad about voicing them any longer.

The first fundamental step in establishing boundaries is **understanding it is okay to have needs and to address them.** You have permission to love yourself. Some of us are so afraid of this idea. We think, *If I give myself an inch, I'll take a mile.*

Or, *If I think I deserve good, that is pride.* Or, *If I am not suffering, I am not like Jesus.*

Scripture says, "Love others as well as *you love yourself*" (Matt. 22:39 MSG). If you can't love *you,* how can you love *them?* You cannot practice externally what you do not receive internally.

This is why it is imperative to accept God's grace, give yourself room, talk kindly to yourself, sit down when your body says to slow down, get away when you need to, accept help, and make room for hearing God.

Boundaries take into account your needs so you can better reach others' needs.

Maybe some of you need to say, "When the door to my room is closed, it means I just need some time alone," or "I am choosing a new diet because I then will have more energy later." Needs get very practical. They address eating, sleeping, proximity to others, and time alone.

Taking care of yourself is not selfish; it is wise.

Two Steps to Cultivate Love

The second foundational step in establishing boundaries is **not working for an outcome but from *your* loved position**.

Another way of saying this is: outcomes belong to the Lord, not us. When we allow outcomes to belong to us, we allow our heart to get caught up in what people want to hear, what they like and fear, and faith wavers. But the truth is, "Victory comes from you, O LORD" (Ps. 3:8).

God handles every result. What do we handle? Going to Him in order to rightfully discern what He wants us to do.

Don't act thoughtlessly, but **understand what the Lord wants you to do**. Don't be drunk with wine, because that will ruin your life. Instead, be filled with the Holy Spirit. (Eph. 5:17–18)

Understanding what God wants you to do allows you to say, "No, God is calling me to spend quality time with my husband in the evening rather than packing pamphlets five nights a week." Or, in another situation, perhaps you decide to talk less on the phone with your friends during the weekends, or you stop looking at that guy's Facebook page all the time because it is making you think the wrong thoughts.

When we make these sorts of decisions, we can wholeheartedly rest in what we've decided. We remember how we are positionally loved, not conditionally loved. God knows our heart's desire. He knows how to best take care of us. He knows we want a good result. The outcome—the victory—belongs to the Lord. Rest there.

The third foundational step in establishing boundaries is to **allow our decisions to pass through the gate of Jesus.**

Jesus said, "I am the gate; whoever enters through me will be saved. They will come in and go out, and *find pasture*" (John 10:9 NIV).

While the gate discussed in this verse certainly refers to Jesus as the gate to eternity, Jesus *is* the Gate. It is who He is. He can help us refuse "to let the world corrupt [us]" (James 1:27) as we thoughtfully discern what He wants us to do.

It may sound like us seeking God by asking:

God, is it Your will that I do this?

God, is it wise for me to step in here?

God, should I take more time to pray about this?

God, how can I protect my heart in this situation?

God, what do You want me to do?

Ask. Seek. Find.

This keeps our flesh and the enemy from exploiting us. It keeps us from "fantasizing" best outcomes. Ones where we believe bad people will suddenly become good. Or ones where we redefine the past and decide we were all wrong, now, so we can't keep the boundaries we've set. Or ones where we decide others have it out for us when they don't.

The Gate helps our thoughts to travel through the heart of God's truth before we act on them. We consider them through the Word of God. We pray about them. We ask God about them. We listen. Otherwise, our flesh and emotions boss us around. Or we dream up an idyllic outcome that will never happen.

The Gate helps us remember that apart from Christ's saving work:

No amount of hopes and dreams can change who our parents are.

No amount of good thoughts can make our drinking husband a non-drinker.

No amount of managing a person can make them better.

No amount of pretending things are okay can actually make them okay.

No amount of catering to someone else's emotions can make things change.

No amount of believing someone is a friend will instantly make them more than an acquaintance.

"'Who has known the mind of the Lord so as to instruct him?' But we have the mind of Christ" (1 Cor. 2:16 NIV). The mind of Christ is ready to instruct us. There is wisdom for us to walk in.

Scripture tells us:

Take heart, because I have overcome the world. (John 16:33)

I have overcome the world. [My conquest is accomplished, **My victory abiding.**] (v. 33 AMP)

If Jesus has overcome—and *is* overcoming—can't He help us with every decision we face?

prayer

Father, I want to know who You say I am, so I care less about what others perceive me to be. I know Your truth, owned as "my truth," is what will unbind me. I know it is Your truth that will set me free from every lie. Help me to secure truth that disassembles lies.

Give me the revelation of You and Your ways that will free me from having to figure everything out, make others do the right thing, show people their way, control emotions, or sign up for more than I can handle. In Jesus's name. Amen.

You Are Already Wanted

I don't know about you, but my heart gets discouraged when it feels unwanted. Sometimes I sign up for things or choose to be part of something just to feel valuable. That is why I picked up the phone to talk to my friend, even though I needed to head out the door. There are many times I want to be wanted. I want to be included. I want to belong. Other times, I do things because I want to do big things for God. I want to feel important, so I take on more.

The truth of the matter is I don't have to look to others to feel wanted. God already proves to me I am wanted. And I don't need to conjure up good works to prove God has good plans for me.

I choose to remember:

- Out of all the billion possible genetic variations at my conception, God could have made someone else but didn't—He chose me.
- God chose me "in Christ" before the foundation of the world (Eph. 1:4).
- God gave me fingerprints and footprints that only I carry.
- God runs to meet me when I make a mistake and gives me His very best, not scraps (remember the prodigal son).
- God fully knows me and still wants me; I am special to Him (Luke 12:7).
- God carefully watches, knows, and observes me (Ps. 139).
- God records every day of my life in a special book (Ps. 139:16).

- God wants to be with me all day long (Isa. 41:10).
- God made me in His image (Gen. 1:27).
- God keeps me as the apple of His eye, because of Jesus (Ps. 17:8).
- God calls me His child.
- God searches the globe for those, like me, who are faithful (2 Chron. 16:9).
- God brings me into His family with Father, Son, and Holy Spirit.

FOURTEEN

executing boundaries

I knew the second I saw the Facebook request that it wouldn't be good. A connection to an old boyfriend is bad news. But what *would* I do?

I knew it went against my values. This should have been a red flag. And, fortunately for me, it was. Listening to my heart, I obeyed the boundary that my husband and I had discussed together. I did not accept the friend request.

Knowing my values and listening to my Gate allowed me to not "shipwreck my faith" by ignoring my conscience. In this, I did not allow my heart to become hardened and thereby allow in further issues (direct messages, profile previews, and so forth). I also did not live with the fear of going against God. I had no guilt later. Instead, I chose to grow trust and respect with my husband; I abided by the good decision we had previously made.

Through boundaries, I made a wise choice to preserve pure love.

The fourth foundational step of boundaries is **being aware of our conscience.**

The aim of our charge is love that issues from a **pure heart** and a good conscience and a sincere faith. (1 Tim. 1:5 ESV)

Where might you feel convicted lately? Have you spent:

- Too much time with a person who keeps hurting your feelings?
- Too much emphasis on a project that should not be monopolizing your time?
- Too much weight on how much you weigh?
- Too much time worrying about what others think of you?
- Too many hours trying to do everything at the expense of your own time with God?
- Too many yeses to things you know will drain you?

To implement boundaries is to regularly start asking yourself a few questions.

1. **How does my heart feel about this?**

    You may need to more deeply consider: Do I constantly get a nagging feeling that I shouldn't be doing something? Do I know that my time here is done, but I feel nervous about stepping away? Do I feel upset and irritated at someone I know I've befriended for too long?

 Example: I knew I needed to stop yelling at my kids in the morning.

2. **Is this right? Good? Helpful? Honoring?**

 Example: I knew being stressed out in the morning as we got ready for school was not good for my kids.

3. **What boundary may I need to set, *now*, around this?**

 Take a second to understand the practical application of boundaries. They can look like:

- telling someone you can only meet from 9:00 to 11:00 a.m. rather than allowing them to expect it will be all day.
- setting a certain amount of time to meet with family.
- only talking about some things and not others with certain people (politics, old issues, and so forth).
- not eating food at midnight hours.
- deciding with your spouse not to text members of the opposite sex.
- letting people know you are unavailable during a specific hour.
- not meeting with a person who, although you talked about it, continues to slight you all the time.
- putting a pretend bubble around yourself so that critical and assaulting words do not penetrate your heart.
- simply saying no.
- communicating your needs.

 Example: I decided to make lunches at night and set out clothes beforehand too. I also decided to have the kids grab their lunchboxes from the counter. This was one less thing for me to do.

4. **How might I need to communicate this new way of doing things?**

You can't change others, but you can communicate your needs and requests. What people do with them is up to them.

Example: I decided to tell my kids my plan to set their lunches on the counter so we'd all be on the same page.

5. **How did this work out for me?**

After going through this process, circle back to ask yourself how things are going, and adjust course as needed. Sometimes you will have to change your plan because it still is not working. Remember, you are responsible for *you and only you.* You are not responsible for other people; you are responsible for your actions.

Example: I couldn't make my kids grab their lunchboxes. But I could put them by the door instead of on the counter, helping them even more.

Try new things. Don't be afraid to adjust course.

Communication Is Key

Paramount to this process is understanding that communication is key. For instance, say you want to have some time to get out and take walks in the late afternoon. Perhaps you need to talk with your husband about your plan so that he can help out with the kids. You might need to call a babysitter. Or you may need to communicate to the kids that they'll need to get their shoes on at five o'clock.

Either way, plan in advance what you will say. My friend, communicator and speaker Mary Steward, says it is always good, when communicating, to:

1. **Begin with compassion.** Recognize who the other person is, what they may be dealing with, and where they are coming from.

2. **Make understanding your goal.** Speak in a way that you can be understood and seek to understand. This may mean talking less, listening more, pausing to consider what they are saying, asking questions, or identifying your main points of communication.

3. **Check your assumptions.** Rather than guessing what the person is thinking or saying, ask the listener if your assumptions are correct. Say, "It appears to me that you feel ____. Is that correct?" Give the person a chance to reply. Avoid taking everything personally.

4. **Cross-communicate expectations.** Be aware of what you want, need, or desire. Make sure your expectations are realistic. Express these needs clearly, directly, and respectfully. Agree upon a course of action for the future.

5. **Mind the small things throughout the conversation.** Use "I" statements. Be brief. Be clear. Honor the other

person and invite them to share their thoughts and feelings. Put your agenda on hold. Find your shared objective and move toward that.

I would also add that it is important to identify roles. For instance, if you are an employee and are talking to the boss, it may not be wise to address them like you would your child. Or to tell your boss what to do. When we realize who we are talking to and rightfully (without fantasies of having a closer relationship than it really is) address them—sister as sister, friend as friend, dad as dad—we will find that our expectations and requests don't get blocked as easily.

Be thoughtful about what you say, and when in doubt, give yourself permission to stop and think.

Everyone needs "room." Offer others time to process. Don't demand they do things your way. Honor their ideas. Open a dialogue. Extend grace. Other people process differently than you do. Recognize other opinions besides your own. Beware of judging others. Hold back critiques.

And be wise—so other people's problems don't become your own.

Beyond this, begin to practice setting speaking limits, taking time to decide, saying no, marking out time for refreshment, and moving with God rather than acting thoughtlessly.

Boundary Checkup

Let's pause and take a breath. How are your boundaries doing? People with good boundaries tend to say things like this:

I really need help with ____.

I will be able to do ____ after I ____.

I am going to let you ____ because I think ____.

I appreciate your understanding that I cannot ____.

I am no longer able to ____, because as much as I might like to, that would cause ____.

I am going to step back because my heart is calling me to a time of rest; I hope you understand.

I am not able to come this time because I am being called elsewhere.

I cannot make a decision today, but I may be able to give you more details on what I am thinking in a week.

I am unable to help now, but maybe I can six months from now.

I am going to need other people to help me.

I cannot help.

I am thankful that you thought of me, but I am doing ____, and as much as I'd like to, doing this would cause me to ____(e.g., feel full of worry, feel like a bad mom).

When Guilt Shows Up

Inevitably, you're going to feel bad about saying no. Or ashamed because others didn't react well. Or like a jerk for standing up for yourself. Or judged when people don't understand. Or bad for doing something new. Or awkward because you asked someone else to do something new.

Maybe you'll even feel prideful because you are going after God's best thing for you. Or uncertain that you made the right decision.

When I feel uncertain—or any of these things, for that matter—I search Scripture. I turn back to folded-down pages and underlined verses to remind myself why I do what I do. I encourage myself to stick it out.

Here are some of the little things that help me to keep on going, to stick it out with boundaries. I hope they encourage you too!

Hopefully, you can rely on these when the going gets tough.

1. Jesus sought what God was doing first.

> Jesus explained, "I tell you the truth, the Son can do **nothing by himself.** He does **only what he sees** the Father doing. Whatever the Father does, the Son also does." (John 5:19)

To "see" here, in the original Greek, means to discern, to behold, or to perceive. Even Jesus perceived from God what to do: "the Son can do *nothing* by himself."

People with Christlike boundaries do what God is calling them to do, independent of what others hope, expect, or demand they do. They listen for and expect the Spirit's

good guidance. Then they walk it out in faith and express
it through love (Gal. 5:6).

> But it was to us that God revealed these things
> by his Spirit. For his Spirit searches out every-
> thing and **shows us God's deep secrets**. No one
> can know a person's thoughts except that person's
> own spirit, and **no one can know God's thoughts
> except God's own Spirit**. And we have received
> God's Spirit (not the world's spirit), so we can
> know the wonderful things God has freely given
> us. (1 Cor. 2:10–12)

2. Jesus knew how people are and positioned His heart accordingly.

> Now when he was in Jerusalem at the Passover
> Feast, many believed in his name when they saw
> the signs that he was doing. But Jesus on his part
> **did not entrust himself to them**, because he knew
> all people and needed no one to bear witness
> about man, for he himself knew what was in man.
> (John 2:23–25 ESV)

Jesus did not twist allegiances or alliances. "No one
needed to tell him about human nature, for he knew
what was in each person's heart" (v. 25). He experienced the people's cheers for Him on Palm Sunday,
then their condemnation five days later. The disciples
pledged to pray for Him outside the garden only to

217

fall asleep later. They declared their loyalty one moment, then deserted Him at the cross.

People say one thing, then do something different. This is not only our problem but a problem with all humankind. Thus, God says, "It is better to take refuge in the LORD than to trust in people" (Ps. 118:8).

People with Christlike boundaries understand: trust God above people, always. Even when it hurts.

3. **Jesus understood that He didn't have to be where He didn't need to be.**

Many times, Jesus pulled away or delayed. Jesus waited four days to go to Lazarus before raising him from the dead. He only healed "a few sick people" even though many more were sick (Mark 6:5). And at one time He left the Pharisees and all their questions and got "back into the boat and . . . crossed to the other side of the lake" (Mark 8:13).

Jesus did not allow people's insistent demands to dictate His heavenly calling. Ultimately, Jesus kept a single-minded focus on His Father's plan. Even to the point of discomfort. Even to the point of people wondering why He did what He did.

When Jesus was entangled with questions, I have not read that He ever over-responded or listed all the reasons why He did what He did. Jesus's words were few, and I bet His pauses between sentences were massive.

Often, more important than knowing *what* to say is knowing what *not* to say. Jesus knew how to not say everything—how to form a response. He also knew how to "slip away."

> But the news about Him was spreading farther, and large crowds kept gathering to hear Him and to be healed of their illnesses. But Jesus Himself would **often slip away** to the wilderness and pray [in seclusion]. (Luke 5:15–16 AMP)

> *People with Christlike boundaries are not afraid to delay or to slip away.*

4. **Jesus took time away to refresh and renew.**

While Jesus might seem like He was all business and no party, as I see it He did take time for Himself. The Bible says Jesus "withdrew to the sea" (Mark 3:7 AMP), "went off to the mountain" (Luke 6:12 AMP), and "often withdrew to the wilderness for prayer" (5:16). Jesus knew the importance of spending time alone to pray and recharge. He also hung out and ate fish with friends.

> Afterward Jesus appeared again to his disciples, by the Sea of Galilee. . . . Then the disciple whom Jesus loved said to Peter, "It is the Lord!" As soon as Simon Peter heard him say, "It is the Lord," he . . . jumped into the water. The other disciples followed in the boat. . . . When they landed, they saw a fire of burning coals there with fish on it, and some bread.

> Jesus said to them, "Bring some of the fish you
> have just caught." So Simon Peter climbed back
> into the boat and dragged the net ashore. . . . Jesus
> said to them, "Come and have breakfast." None of
> the disciples dared ask him, "Who are you?" They
> knew it was the Lord. Jesus came, took the bread
> and gave it to them, and did the same with the fish.
> This was now the third time Jesus appeared to his
> disciples after he was raised from the dead. (John
> 21:1, 7–14)

In this, recreation was reconciliation (especially for Peter). There are purposes in recreation of rest and deeper relationship.

People with Christlike boundaries know refreshment can mean renewed relationships.

5. **Jesus, in many cases, does not do for people what they can do for themselves.**

John 5 tells the story of an incapacitated man who had lain on a mat for thirty-eight years. Jesus, with wisdom, asked him, "Do you want to get well?" (v. 6).

The man replied, "I can't. . . . I have no one to put me into the pool when the water bubbles up. Someone else always gets there ahead of me" (v. 7).

The man had excuses. Jesus had none.

Jesus said, "Stand up, pick up your mat, and walk!" (v. 8). Jesus gave the man an opportunity to take action. The man picked up his mat to partner with Jesus's healing.

And the man got up and walked! The man had a part to do in his healing. But many don't even want to be healed.

People with Christlike boundaries, in many cases, should not insist on rescuing someone who doesn't want a rescue. Likewise, they should reconsider helping a person who wants no help.

6. Jesus endured awkwardness.

> Some people brought a blind man and begged Jesus to touch him. He took the blind man by the hand and led him outside the village. When he had **spit on the man's eyes** and put his hands on him, Jesus asked, "Do you see anything?" (Mark 8:22–23)

Yes. Jesus spit on a man's face.

People with Christlike boundaries understand that enduring awkwardness is part of being a Christian. What God calls us to do often does not make sense to our flesh. But obedience trumps our flesh.

7. Jesus made room for joy.

Many of us know Jesus as a "man of sorrows, acquainted with deepest grief" (Isa. 53:3), yet He also was acquainted with joy.

At that time Jesus, **full of joy through the Holy Spirit**, said, "I praise you, Father, Lord of heaven and earth." (Luke 10:21 NIV)

I have told you these things so that you will be **filled with my joy.** Yes, your joy will overflow! (John 15:11)

People with Christlike boundaries don't always down-play their joy; they realize joy is a gift from God and a fruit of the Spirit. They understand the contagious nature of joy that has the power to uplift others.

8. **Jesus did not have to see heavenly impact to know it was happening.**

When Jesus had entered Capernaum, a centurion came to him, asking for help. "Lord," he said, "my servant lies at home paralyzed, suffering terribly."

Jesus said to him, "Shall I come and heal him?"

The centurion replied, "Lord, I do not deserve to have you come under my roof. But just say the word, and my servant will be healed. For I myself am a man under authority, with soldiers under me. I tell this one, 'Go,' and he goes; and that one, 'Come,' and he comes. I say to my servant, 'Do this,' and he does it."

When Jesus heard this, he was amazed and said to those following him, "Truly I tell you, I have not found anyone in Israel with such great faith." (Matt. 8:5–13 NIV)

People with Christlike boundaries don't have to see with their eyes to believe God is moving. They are people of great faith. They know that God saves more than their abilities or strategies ever will.

9. **Jesus was honest about His needs and wants.**

Remember the man who got spit in his eyes? After he was healed, Jesus said to him, "Don't even go into the village" (Mark 8:26).

So many times, Jesus told people what He needed them to do, such as to go to a certain place, to not go somewhere, to be quiet, or to tell everyone they met what He had done.

As a person of boundaries, you may have to:

- Redefine how much time you can spend with a person.
- Relocate.
- Respond with different words.
- Relieve yourself of pressures you've been carrying by asking for help, restructuring your participation, or bringing in other people.
- React with the word *no*.
- Remove yourself from a given situation.
- Release a role you thought you "had to do."
- Reach out to a friend to help you.

- Reprioritize your time or money.
- Reevaluate who you should be in relationship with.
- Recognize that it is time for a new direction.
- Request time, space, or help.
- Remove the burden to respond right away.
  People with good boundaries do "a new thing."

As I see it, Jesus did not permit Himself to be pulled a million directions at one time. As a man of focus, He was a man of impact. Likewise, the more we keep focus on God and His small callings, the more we impact others. Here, our faith learns to express itself through love. Pure love.

And there's no greater rest than the wholehearted joy found in serving and ministering unto the Lord.

prayer

God, I thank You for Jesus. Truly, I have all I need for godliness, life, and contentment. My life is so full, in You. Teach me wisdom. Direct me in all Your ways. Immerse me in Your love. Lead me in rest, so that I can pour out love, joy, peace, patience, kindness, goodness, gentleness, and self-control. Oh, how I love You. You are amazing. In Jesus's name. Amen.

A Little Note on Grace

Undoubtedly, we all fall along our way. We set out with high and lofty intentions of doing great and then trip up. We set boundaries and then stumble. The question is not, Will we fall? The question is, How will we deal with it when we do?

The answer of how we deal with our mess-ups has a whole lot to do with grace.

To me, "cheap grace" is anything less than "rich grace." I've noticed that I can never receive too much grace; however, I can receive too little. Anytime I lessen its value, I do it a disservice. I make it cheap. I lessen what Jesus has done on the cross for me.

Here, I feel kind of forgiven, kind of okay, and kind of free of condemnation. I resort to making self-help plans and dedicate my life to holding up a magnifying glass against my every move as I walk out a sin-management program for all my days. The goal here is to keep myself righteous and out of shame and guilt.

It never works.

Yet when I receive "rich grace," I notice I am immediately free. I am wholly forgiven. The pain of what I did disappears. Completely. In light of God's glory and grace because of the price Jesus paid. My lesser work fades in comparison to His greater work. And it's *done*. Really done. Finally done.

Because I've been forgiven much, I can love much. Because I've received much grace, I find grace to help me walk a new way. I get free. The sin that once entangled me no longer has enough rope to hang me anymore. It's profound.

When you mess up, do too much, or find yourself overwhelmed, I encourage you to accept "rich grace." Then, step right back on the path that God has for you.

I tell you, her sins—and they are many—have been forgiven, so she has shown me much love. But a person who is forgiven little shows only little love. (Luke 7:47)

conclusion

ENCOURAGEMENT
AS YOU GO ON YOUR WAY

Peace is *now*.

It is here. You don't have to wait for rest any longer. Jesus has given you everything you need for life and godliness. The hard work is done. Now is the time for you to carry an easy yoke.

With this said, my greatest hope for you is that you habitually and continually walk with God. He is ever near. Closer than you know. More present than you think. More ready to help you than you are likely aware.

May you stay with Him in everything. May you perceive and receive His peace, joy, and life.

Jesus is your rest. Christ in you is your hope of glory. No matter what you do, where you go, or who you are with, you can "come away with God," doing all things with Him, unto

Him, and because of Him. Allow your heart to thrive and be fully alive.

Things like reading, talking with a friend, sitting in nature, taking a walk, listening to music, or taking a bath are good for your soul. They are needed. Don't forgo them. At the same time, remember: they aren't full and complete rest.

They're short-lived.

The dog barks during your reading time, and you remember you have to feed him. A phone call interrupts your time to sit down, so you get up. A mail carrier comes to the door, and you remember three other things you have to do. Time runs out; you stress until you can do them again.

People who live for *short-term* hardly ever get rested. They spend their lives wanting to be somewhere else. Living for the future. Waiting for the next rest-fix . . . and absent from the place they're currently at.

But, as you've come to see in this book, God is our greatest destination of rest. God *with us.* He is with us at work. With us in our commute. With us in our five free minutes that we have as we sit on the couch. To walk with Him is to walk in rest.

Long-lasting soul rest, beyond momentary rest, is the rhythm of connecting and conversing with God.

Long-lasting rest fills. It restores. It endures. It comes from the inside out more than the outside in. It is not dependent on external conditions—what people do, say, or think—but remains internally constant. It is the filling of the Holy Spirit. It is deep connectedness to Christ in you, the hope of glory.

Long-lasting rest also nourishes. It protects your soul. It keeps you faithful. From this vantage point, it's far easier to see what God is doing rather than what He is not doing.

From this place comes a deep knowing, for children of God, that they are positionally loved more than they are conditionally loved. They remember that God is their

1. **Constant defender.** It is not our bow or sword that saves but He who gives victory over enemies (Ps. 44:6–7).

2. **Advancing protector.** It is by His right hand and not your arm that victory comes (Ps. 44:3).

3. **True love.** God loves us with an everlasting love, drawing us in with lovingkindness (Jer. 31:3).

For those who rest, God's truths sink deep.

Preserving Long-Lasting Soul Rest

This is not to say that the enemy of our soul won't lie to us again. He may come around the corner and tell you things like:

If you rest, nothing that needs to get done will be taken care of. You need to be doing more stuff. You can't waste time sitting down with God.

You're too late and you'll never live out your purpose, especially if you waste time on yourself.

You've made mistakes too big for God to handle.

People are judging you for looking like you are "doing nothing."

I want you to know, in these cases, that you are not without a defense. You can immediately recover rest. But you may want to consider:

Confessing your sin and turning a new way.

Declaring that God still wants you.

Thanking Jesus for all He's done.

Walking in obedience again, because this is a main thoroughfare of rest.

Forgiving those who need forgiving.

Reminding yourself of who you are in Christ Jesus (chosen, wanted, loved, a new creation).

Worshiping with all your heart.

Praising God's name again.

We can return to Jesus anytime. There is always a way out of temptation and a way back to rest. We can "be still, and know that [He is] God" (Ps. 46:10).

God is greater than anything you face.

God is mightier than anything you come up against.

Christ is worthy all the time.

You are His daughter every day.

You are free because Christ has set you free.

You are loved to love.

Jesus is with you. Breathe Him in, deeply. Resolutely fight to hold Him near. Remember all He has accomplished for you. Live in love and obedience.

This will make others take notice. They will say things like, "Wow. You don't just speak religious words, you live them." Let your life shine as an authentic, impactful living testimony of Jesus.

And when you fail? Or mess up? Let go of the fact that you are imperfect. Confess. Get up. Learn. Grow. Seek God. Let Him transform you. And keep going.

Now that all is said and done within these pages, I release you with the great hope that you will live out abounding joy and peace.

I know you are in good hands. The Good Shepherd has a tight hold of your life. And I feel confident that He'll lead you to streams of blue rivers and green pastures of rest and renewal, just like the cover on this book. In this place you can know, deeply, that God takes care of you. My prayer is that you stay there. And that I'll stay there too.

And in all this rest, with love abounding, what can you do with the joy in your heart? You can give thanks to God. He is the giver of every good gift. Speak forth from your heart praise and thanks.

God, my shepherd!
> I don't need a thing.
You have bedded me down in lush meadows,
> you find me quiet pools to drink from.
True to your word,
> you let me catch my breath
> and send me in the right direction.

Even when the way goes through
> Death Valley,
I'm not afraid
> when you walk at my side.
Your trusty shepherd's crook
> makes me feel secure.

You serve me a six-course dinner
> right in front of my enemies.
You revive my drooping head;
> my cup brims with blessing.

Your beauty and love chase after me
> every day of my life.
I'm back home in the house of God
> for the rest of my life. (Ps. 23 MSG)

May the Sabbath rest of Jesus consume you all of your days!

Prayer

Father God, You meet my every need. You are my every hope.
You are my very life. You provide the air that fills me. You

keep me alive. You hold the world together. You can more than hold the details of my life together. I thank You that You are the Shepherd of my soul, my life, and my future. I rest in that today. I trust Your good, perfect, and pleasing will for my life. You are good.

I trust You in all things, all the time, and in every way. I trust You to lead me to rest. To guide me to pastures of peace. To lead me to springs of life. I thank You for Your care.

Please show me when, where, and how to stop when I need to. Even more, give me the ability to continually give You my burdens and my care, Father. I don't want to carry them anymore. They don't help me; they hinder me. I don't want to be tied down to them. I don't want to be held back in my coming days. You offer me a better way.

Help me to rightfully discern, understand, and hear Your heart for me, in all my ways. Lead me according to Your will, and may I bring the fullness of You with me at all times. I love You. I thank You for all You taught me as I read this book. I ask for a heavenly power to be able to implement what I have learned here, so a life of rest might truly be mine.

And, most of all, I praise Jesus for the fullness of the work on the cross.

In Jesus's name. Amen.

How to Go Forward into Rest

For your plan to succeed, you first need to have one. What is your plan? What will you focus on? What boundaries are necessary? How will you see them through?

Consider what God has stirred up in your heart throughout this book. Don't let that idea or revelation pass. Give it a permanent place within you. Allow it to become significant. Permit it to change your life.

Write out your plan here:

_____

_____

_____

_____

Get free daily prayers, Scripture encouragement cards, and practical ideas on ways you can rest! Visit www.restnowbook.com for these tools and others.

group study questions

Introduction

1. What does your struggle to rest look like?
2. What are you hoping to gain from this book?
3. What area in your life most needs rest and recovery?
4. Do you believe God has a heart to meet you there? Why or why not?

Bible verse to ponder: Psalm 55:6

Chapter 1: Our Endless Pursuit of More

1. In what ways do you seek "the endless pursuit of more"?
2. How has all this pursuing hurt you?

3. We specified some life activities that are *not* rest. Did any of these resonate with you? Why?

4. What do you believe is the difference between "physical rest" and "soul rest"?

5. What did God stir up in your heart in this chapter? What can you do about it?

Bible verse to ponder: John 3:30

Chapter 2: What Is Your Truth?

1. Do you feel afraid to share your truth with others? Why?

2. How have you held truth back? Share an example.

3. What does it mean if people see you as you are?

4. What are some of your simple truths?

5. What do you think God says about them?

6. Share in your group what you think happens in relationship when we are honest with each other.

Bible verses to ponder: Colossians 3:9–10

Chapter 3: How You Think

1. What were your parents like when you were a child?

2. Where have you felt hurt, neglected, or left behind?

3. How do you fear this will happen again? How do you project this fear onto others?

4. What sort of good Father is God? How does He transcend all your earthly definitions of a parent?

5. Do you live as conditionally loved or positionally loved? How can you begin to move so you can rest under your new position in Christ Jesus, which is *loved?*

Bible verses to ponder: 1 John 4:16–18

Chapter 4: Recovering Prayer

1. What are some of your unanswered prayers? Were any of them worked out later? Did you find good in the bad?

2. What prayers has God answered in a miraculous way?

3. What reasons most resonate in your heart with why there may be "prayer delays"?

4. How can you begin to pray again? Where? When? How?

5. What is most on your heart? Can you begin, right now, by praying for that?

Bible verse to ponder: Colossians 4:2

Chapter 5: The Way of Weakness

1. Where do you feel weak?

2. What do you think God says about this weakness?

3. How do you think about your feelings? Are they good? Bad? Troublesome?

4. What does it mean for Christ's power to flow through you?

5. How does professing and embracing your weakness help others?

6. What is God calling you to right now?

Bible verse to ponder: Psalm 34:8

Chapter 6: The Way of Humility

1. How do you judge?

2. Do you ever feel like you take a know-it-all or fix-it-all attitude? How does that look in your life?

3. What pharisaic tendencies may you have?

4. When have you judged someone and been wrong? How have you come to see the log in your own eye?

5. What does humility mean to you?

6. What inspired you from this chapter?

7. How can you support those around you from a pure heart, not a works-based one?

Bible verses to ponder: 1 Corinthians 3:18–20 (MSG)

Chapter 7: The Way of Forgiveness

1. How does unforgiveness hurt us?

2. Why do we not forgive?

3. Why do you think we are called as Christians to forgive so quickly?

4. What can happen in our relationships when we forgive?

5. What sort of release may be available to us after we forgive?

6. Who do you need to forgive? Have you forgiven them?

Bible verse to ponder: Matthew 6:15

Chapter 8: The Way of Focus

1. Where do you lose focus?

2. What sort of distractions make focusing on God hard?

3. How could deep work help you?

4. What would a life of meaning look like to you? How can you foster that?

5. What sort of sacrifices would you have to make? What sort of gains might you find?

Bible verses to ponder: Philippians 3:13–14

Chapter 9: The Way of Less

1. When has *more* not made you happy?

2. Why did you think it would?

3. Why does having less actually lead to more fulfillment?

4. If Jesus called you to leave it all, could you?

5. What do you feel attached to?

6. What was God stirring up in your heart as you read this chapter?

Bible verses to ponder: Hebrews 13:5–6 MSG

Chapter 10: The Way of Words

1. Do you speak words of hope or words of doubt and complaint?

2. How do your words impact others and your world?

3. How could you begin to think about and change your words?

4. How have words impacted your life?

5. How do words lead to rest? Has a word from someone else ever provided you rest?

Bible verse to ponder: Proverbs 18:20

Chapter 11: The Way of Christ in Us

1. Is God's grace enough? How has your life showed that you have believed this? Not believed this?

2. What does it look like to take care of yourself?

3. Is there a difference between momentary rest and soul rest? What is it?

4. How can you say no to what hinders moments of recovery for you?

5. How could rest-in-action look in your world, if you were to define it?

Bible verse to ponder: Psalm 4:8

Chapter 12: What Boundaries Are and Are Not

1. Where do you feel people take advantage of you?

2. What are your initial thoughts about boundaries? How do they make you feel?

3. How might you have gotten boundaries wrong in the past?

4. What sorts of relationships may need boundaries?

5. Why do boundaries help in relationships? What could you gain?

Bible verses to ponder: Psalm 91:1–2

Chapter 13: The Heart of Boundaries

1. How do well-meaning people suck you into things?

2. Are you ever afraid to say no? Why?

3. How can you remember that God has plans for you and that you are significant?

4. What are some of your needs? How can you more clearly meet them?

5. Why does God care about your needs? Why does He want you to love yourself?

Bible verse to ponder: Colossians 3:23

Chapter 14: Executing Boundaries

1. What do you feel convicted of? What is your conscience saying? Revealing?

2. Where may you *not* be doing what is good, honorable, or honoring?

3. What are some practical actions you need to take or lines you need to draw in your life?

4. How can you communicate in a new way? Who do you need to put this into action with?

5. How can you plan to stick to your boundaries? What might you come up against?

6. How does Jesus encourage you to enforce boundaries?

Bible verse to ponder: Galatians 6:5

Conclusion: Encouragement as You Go on Your Way

1. How can you forge long-lasting soul rest into your life?

2. What tries to steal it? How can you preemptively plan against that?

3. Where do you want to be free? What would soul rest in this area look like?

4. How could boundaries help reinforce your rest-keeping?

5. What is God calling you to do or to move out in, at this point?

Bible verses to ponder: Psalm 23 MSG

acknowledgments

God made me rest. "He *makes me* lie down in green pastures, he leads me beside quiet waters" (Ps. 23:2 NIV). Through rejection, discouragement, and fear, in many ways, God *made me* sit down with Him. There, next to Him, I found true rest. He made me go deeper. I saw what I didn't want to see. I learned how I was relying on people and not God. Although I didn't always welcome it, I am now thankful for God's mandated rest in my life.

In any case, many people have spoken into my discovery of rest. My husband, Emanuel, encourages me to seek God, again and again. My mom and dad remind me of simple truths. My kids, Michael and Madison, tell me I can do it and pray for me. My friends, namely Julie, Mercy, Sylvia, Mia, Dawn, and Mary, let me speak raw truths.

Kaity Walters, my son's third-grade teacher, shared a story that landed in this book. Mary, whom I once felt jealous of, taught me a lesson on communication that was so wise. I love her now more than ever. Karen Mortensen, a pastoral counselor, gave me much insight about boundaries. Joanna Weaver, Julie Stephens, and, of course, Emanuel Balarie prayed for me at key moments.

Baker Books believes in me. Every person on the team is a flexible team player. They love me and I love them. What a fantastic publisher! Amanda Luedeke, my literary agent, you not only make me laugh but you work with me throughout the process. The little things make all the difference. And you help me. Thank you, Nicci, for editing my book; I am grateful for your patience.

There's not much else to say, other than God is good. I pray He gets all the glory from this book, and that I give Him all of my heart for all the days of my life. I love You, Father, Son, and Holy Spirit! It is great to do life with You!

notes

Chapter 1 Our Endless Pursuit of More

1. Maurie Backman, "It's Official: Most Americans Are Currently in Debt," *The Motley Fool,* February 15, 2018, https://www.fool.com/retirement/2018/02/15/its-official-most-americans-are-currently-in-debt.aspx.

2. Elizabeth Renter, "2019 Holiday Shopping Report," *Nerd Wallet,* November 6, 2019, https://www.nerdwallet.com/blog/2019-holiday-shopping-report/.

3. Allyson Chiu, "Americans Are the Unhappiest They've Ever Been, U.N. Report Finds: An 'Epidemic of Addictions' Could Be to Blame," *The Washington Post,* March 21, 2019, https://www.washingtonpost.com/nation/2019/03/21/americans-are-unhappiest-theyve-ever-been-un-report-finds-an-epidemic-addictions-could-be-blame/?noredirect=on.

4. Gemma Mullin, "The Great Depression: Americans Are among Most Negative People on Earth, New Survey Reveals," *The Sun,* April 29, 2019, https://www.thesun.co.uk/news/8960855/americans-most-negative-people-on-earth/.

Chapter 2 What Is Your Truth?

1. "UMass Amherst Researcher Finds Most People Lie in Everyday Conversation," June 10, 2002, University of Massachusetts Amherst, https://www.umass.edu/newsoffice/article/umass-amherst-researcher-finds-most-people-lie-everyday-conversation.

2. Christian Jarrett, "The 'Beautiful Mess' Effect: Other People View Our Vulnerability More Positively Than We Do," *Research Digest,* accessed March

2, 2020, https://digest.bps.org.uk/2018/08/02/the-beautiful-mess-effect
-other-people-view-our-vulnerability-more-positively-than-we-do/.

Chapter 3 How You Think

1. Lisa Wingate, *Before We Were Yours* (New York: Ballantine, 2017), 248.

Chapter 5 The Way of Weakness

1. Merriam-Webster, s.v. "shame," accessed March 4, 2020, https://www
.merriam-webster.com/dictionary/shame.

2. Alison Escalante, "U.S. Leads in the Worldwide Anxiety Epidemic," *Psychology Today*, April 26, 2019, https://www.psychologytoday.com/us/blog
/shouldstorm/201904/us-leads-in-the-worldwide-anxiety-epidemic; Karen
Kaplan, "It's Not Just You, We're All Living in the United States of Anxiety,"
Los Angeles Times, May 8, 2018, https://www.latimes.com/science/science
now/la-sci-sn-americans-more-anxious-20180508-story.html.

Chapter 6 The Way of Humility

1. David Jeremiah, "Galatians 6:7–9," *The Jeremiah Study Bible: What It
Says, What It Means*, NIV ed. (Franklin, TN: Worthy, 2016).

Chapter 7 The Way of Forgiveness

1. R. Morgan Griffin, "10 Health Problems Related to Stress That You Can
Fix," WebMD, accessed March 5, 2020, https://www.webmd.com/balance
/stress-management/features/10-fixable-stress-related-health-problems#1.

2. Merriam-Webster, s.v. "defile," accessed March 5, 2020, https://www
.merriam-webster.com/dictionary/defile.

3. R. T. Kendall, *Total Forgiveness* (Lake Mary, FL: Charisma House,
2007), 48.

Chapter 8 The Way of Focus

1. Gavin Francis, "Irresistible: Why We Can't Stop Checking, Scrolling,
Clicking and Watching (Review)," *The Guardian*, February 26, 2017, https://
www.theguardian.com/books/2017/feb/26/irresistible-why-cant-stop
-checking-scrolling-clicking-adam-alter-review-internet-addiction.

2. Cal Newport, *Deep Work* (New York: Hachette, 2016), 2. See also Cal
Newport, "Deep Work," *Cal Newport* (blog), accessed April 15, 2020, https://
www.calnewport.com/books/deep-work/.

Chapter 9 The Way of Less

1. Daniel Kurt, "Are You in the World's Top 1 Percent?" *Investopedia*, September 25, 2019, https://www.investopedia.com/articles/personal-fin ance/050615/are-you-top-one-percent-world.asp.

Chapter 10 The Way of Words

1. Global News, "IKEA Conducts Bullying Experiment on Plants—the Results Are Shocking," *Global News*, May 18, 2018, https://globalnews.ca /news/4217594/bully-a-plant-ikea/.

Chapter 11 The Way of Christ in Us

1. R. A. Torrey, "The Works of the Holy Spirit in Jesus Christ," Bible Hub, accessed March 10, 2020, https://biblehub.com/library/torrey/the_person _and_work_of_the_holy_spirit/chapter_xxii_the_work_of.htm.

Kelly Balarie is the author of *Fear Fighting* and *Battle Ready.* When speaking at women's conferences around the nation, Kelly delights in seeing lives transformed when God moves mountains in people's lives. Beyond speaking, Kelly has been seen on *TODAY, The 700 Club,* Crosswalk.com, iBelieve.com, and (in)courage. Her work has also been featured by *Relevant* and *Today's Christian Woman.* She lives with her husband and two kiddos on the East Coast. Join Kelly on her blog, www.purposefulfaith.com.

YOU CAN LIVE
VICTORIOUSLY.

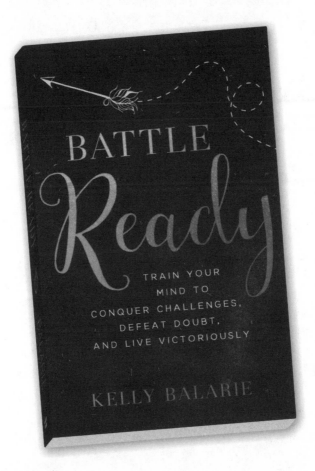

Battle Ready is a hands-on scriptural plan that teaches you twelve easy-to-implement, confidence-building mindsets designed to transform your thoughts and, therefore, your life.

Connect with Kelly!

For more information and online resources, visit

RestNowBook.com

and

PurposefulFaith.com